Standardized Testing Skills

Strategies, Techniques, Activities To Help Raise Students' Scores

Guinevere Durham

ROWMAN & LITTLEFIELD EDUCATION
A division of
ROWMAN & LITTLEFIELD
Lanham • Boulder • New York • Toronto • Plymouth, UK

Published by Rowman & Littlefield Education
A division of Rowman & Littlefield
4501 Forbes Boulevard, Suite 200, Lanham, Maryland 20706
www.rowman.com

10 Thornbury Road, Plymouth PL6 7PP, United Kingdom

British Library Cataloguing in Publication Information Available

Library of Congress Cataloging-in-Publication Data

Durham, Guinevere, 1937-
Standardized testing skills : strategies, techniques, activities to help raise students' scores / Guinevere
Durham.
p. cm.
Includes bibliographical references.
ISBN 978-1-61048-994-2 (cloth : alk. paper) -- ISBN 978-1-61048-995-9 (pbk. : alk. paper) -- ISBN
978-1-61048-996-6 (electronic)
1. Test-taking skills--Study and teaching. 2. Educational tests and measurements. I. Title.
LB3060.57.D86 2014
371.26--dc 3

2013045615

∞ ™ The paper used in this publication meets the minimum requirements of American
National Standard for Information Sciences Permanence of Paper for Printed Library
Materials, ANSI/NISO Z39.48-1992.

Printed in the United States of America

OTHER BOOKS ON TESTING BY RLE

Contents

Contents

Chapter One

Test-Wiseness: What, When, Why, and How

The word *test* generates physical, mental, and emotional reactions in people who hear it and have to comply. These reactions are magnified in the students in our schools.

Three factors have a bearing on how well one does on a test: "1.) Knowledge of the material, 2.) Test anxiety, and 3.) Test-wiseness."[1] As for the first item, the vast majority of teachers are dedicated professionals who effectively teach the knowledge of the material. Parents also supplement and support what the student learns in the classroom.

The second factor, test anxiety, is familiar to all students. The physical ailments are the most obvious: sweaty palms, butterflies in the stomach, headaches, loss of appetite or excess appetite, and loss of sleep. Then there is the worry factor. The bright students worry about maintaining their As and their rank in class, while the struggling students worry about passing. They all worry about what would happen if they forgot everything and did poorly. Additional stress is placed on the student when getting a specific score dictates whether the student is promoted to the next grade, passes the class, gets into the college of choice, or obtains a scholarship.

The third factor, test-wiseness (also called test-taking skills), is the set of past experiences and techniques that the test taker brings to the test. It is also the person's familiarity with the format of the test. These experiences, techniques, and familiarity with the format are the "test-taking skills" taught to the student by teachers and parents. Elementary school children, being new to the testing situation, have not had enough years in the education system to acquire test-wiseness. They also do not have the luxury of time in which to learn these skills.

An example of how learning test-taking skills can increase a student's score is the following experience of a new second grade teacher. The teacher was giving the reading comprehension section of the test. She was allowed to read the general directions twice and also to read directions of specific skills. The question was one on sequence. She knew her students could read or hear a story and then number four sentences in the correct sequential order about the passage. Then she saw how the problem was written on the test. She anticipated the reaction she received.

The direction read by the teacher (twice) was, "Choose the correct order of the group of sentences below. On your answer sheet, mark the letter of the sentence order that is correct."

This is what the eight-year-olds were looking at in the test booklet:

1. Mary put chocolate icing on the cake.
2. Mary got out the cake mix and bowls.
3. Mary put the cake into the oven.
4. Mary mixed the cake and put it into the pan.
A. 3, 1, 4, 2
B. 4, 3, 2, 1
C. 2, 4, 3, 1
D. 2, 1, 3, 4

In the test booklet, the correct answer for the student to bubble in was "C." Five students in the class of thirty bubbled in the correct answer; three of them had a lucky guess. In tests for higher grades, the students were required to put six sentences in the proper order.

After the completed tests were sent in to the company that machine-scored them, the teacher taught the students the format. She continued to teach this format every school year with good results for her efforts.

The purpose of this book is to provide teachers and parents with the theory, strategies, and techniques effective in teaching test-taking skills to the students, thus creating test-wise test-takers. A seasoned elementary principal instilled in his new, young teachers the adage "do not assume." This book is written with that in mind: do not assume that your students know how to take a test, no matter what the grade level.

Many studies have been conducted that verify the necessity of teaching test-taking skills to students. Research also shows that the test-taking skills should be reviewed and new ones taught for each new grade level. Do not assume that because the skills were taught the previous school year, the student will remember them in their current grade.

The need for teaching test-taking skills has been researched for well over fifty years. These early studies were innovative at the time. But, since the inception of the No Child Left Behind Act in 2002, research in this area has both increased in activity and been explored by school systems across the country. The experts may be unknown to readers of this book, but their findings tend to mirror each other. Test-taking skills are a necessity for every curriculum.

The information has sparked school systems to add this skill to their curriculum in every grade level. Many school systems purchase commercial programs, either in software or workbook form. The skills are taught as an entity unto themselves. For elementary students, this may be ineffective because they have not as yet developed the skills to transfer the test-taking skills information to the actual curriculum of reading, math, social studies, or science. This book demonstrates how to teach the skills in conjunction with the area subject matter while using the textbooks required by any school system.

Researchers in this field are predominantly educators, psychologists, and psychiatrists. Also in agreement by researchers is that teaching test-taking skills will increase the student's score. That does not mean that the student will "ace" the test. What it does mean is that the test score will reflect the student's true academic potential. By teaching test-taking skills, we can help students overcome test anxiety and raise their score between 10 and 20 percent, depending on the research study.

POINTS TO REMEMBER

- Tests, such as the SAT and the ACT, are designed to measure knowledge acquired over a long period of time. Cramming doesn't help; in fact, it usually increases anxiety.
- Research has shown that test takers who have been taught test-taking skills score 10 to 20 percent higher than they would have without the training. [2]
- Anxiety has lowered more test scores than does a lack of the knowledge of the material.
- We are programmed from childhood about the "extreme" importance of tests, thus the source of the anxiety.
- Successful musicians and athletes do not perform with unfamiliar "gear." The "gear" of the tests is the style, the format, and the proper writing implements.
- Successful musicians and athletes do not perform without practice. Practice test taking by completing practice tests and the sample questions before each section.

Teach this acronym to students and remind them to repeat it in their minds before and during each test: WATCH.

Watch the signs, particularly in math
Allow enough time; that is, pace yourself

Two directions: listen and read twice
Check key words
Hop over what you don't know. Remember to come back to it later.

Chapter Two

The State Criterion Referenced Testing of Students

Standardized tests have been used in schools for years. These tests usually were in the form of nationally normed achievement tests. They did what they said they would do—that is, test what students knew. These tests were one tool in the scheme of a student's education. The results were used along with the student's accumulative year's work to decide upon promotion or retention.

But the tests did not test what the students at each grade level had been taught through their textbooks used in their school system. All students around the country were taught the same curriculum, but, depending on the textbook series, the skills were not taught in the same sequence of grade level or time in the school year. The scoring system ranked the students with their peers, not a pass or fail grade.

Then came the "accountability movement," the outgrowth of which resulted in the No Child Left Behind Act of 2000. The goal of the law was that every student would perform on or above grade level. In 2001, states were charged with creating their standards and the tests to measure these standards.

In 2009, the law was changed to Race for the Top. At that time, a new set of standards were developed, called Common Core Standards. All but five states concurred with these standards, and they set about to revise their tests accordingly.

Everyone was accountable, from the state boards of education down to the classroom teacher. The stress and pressure shifted to the students. They were subjected to experiences in the testing agenda that were very new to them. The bad news was, "These elementary children felt as if the weight of the world was on their shoulders." The good news is, "School level educators and parents have risen to the occasion and are working hard to teach, mentor, and support these young students."

This book will not go in depth into the laws, the mandates, nor the implementation process. Nor will it discuss the pros and cons, positives and negatives, or successes or failures of the laws. It will speak to the status of the programs, the states' role, and how the educators (classroom up through state level) and parents can and will teach and support the young students in meeting the challenges.

The standards of 2001 were redeveloped for kindergarten through grade twelve. The next step was to recreate, or purchase nationally, the tests that would determine whether or not the students had mastered the required skills. Many states assembled teams of experts to develop the instrument that would meet their needs for testing, while others found nationally developed tests that met their needs. The state test developing teams consisted of state-level curriculum and assessment specialists, school system–level specialists in all areas, and classroom teachers. Writing valid test items is a monumental and time-consuming task. For the tests to be valid, the test questions had to measure the skills that were being taught in the classrooms, the Common Core Standards.

The tests were called criterion referenced tests. This type of test is written to measure knowledge of a specific subject—that is, spelling, addition and subtraction, reading comprehension, etc. They measure whether or not the student has mastered specific material. The students are not ranked with other students. Three characteristics are common to criterion referenced tests:

- They measure mastery of specific subject matter.
- They measure the results of the instruction.
- Their scores are judged by a specific standard or criteria. Seventy percent, or seven out of ten, was considered a passing score.

In a norm referenced achievement test, the norms are based on the actual performance of students in a specific grade or age group. These scores represent average or typical performance of the group; they are not regarded as standards. The students are ranked with others in the same group. There is no pass or fail. Scores are in percentiles, stanines, or grade equivalent.

These normed referenced achievement tests answer the question, "How is this student doing in relationship to the peer group?" The criterion referenced tests answer the question, "What can this student do?" or "Has the student learned what was taught in the classroom?"

A nationally developed achievement test is a general measure of what is being taught in a particular grade level (e.g., third, fourth, etc.) or a specific subject area classroom (e.g., science, social studies, math, etc.). The test creators base their items or questions on information in textbooks, state sylla-buses, and other curriculum material from around the country. Thus, these tests are assessing general information. The scores are not pass/fail; they are in percentiles, ranking students among their peers.

The results were not always a true indication of "did the student learn what was taught from the textbooks in the classroom?" The results were not necessarily an assessment of the student's true potential. Teachers became very resourceful. In one county school system, the national tests were given sometime during the month of April. In the fifth grade, fractions were taught in May. The students did not score well on that part of the test. These teachers began teaching fractions out of sequence in their curriculum. They believed it was not fair to test students on material they had not been taught yet. Their strategy worked. Math scores went up.

For the new state criterion referenced tests, each state developed its own sequence of Common Core Standards and then created the tests to measure the mastery of the skills. A valid test score is the result. To best teach and support the students, both parents and school-level educators need to be apprised of the syllabus and the standards that will be tested. When asking for this document, parents and educators should be aware that it may have any number of titles, grade-level expectations, curriculum continuum, and pupil progression plans, to name a few. There are four sources that will provide this information:

- The director of elementary curriculum, director of elementary education, or director of assessment of the school system not only will have a copy, but most likely will have been instrumental in helping to write it. It may be in print form or on their website. When asking for it, be specific as to which grade level or high school class you need.
- At the school level, the school principal, curriculum coordinator, or class-room teacher is the source for the information. These folks are the best source to explain it to the parent. They also know which skills are priori-tized and which are supportive. The document may be in print form or on the school's website.
- Each state department of education has a website that will also have this information available to parents and teachers for kindergarten through high school curriculum. The subjects tested are reading, language arts (English grammar), math, social studies, and science. These sites also offer practice tests in all areas. Because the tests given to students are in paper/pencil format, print out the practice tests for the student's use. The answers to the practice tests are also on the website. This is a valuable teaching tool for it tells not only what the correct response is and why, it tells why each incorrect response is the wrong choice. This website also

gives information about the dates of each test. (See appendix B for web addresses.)

- The fourth source is the website www.EDinformatics.com/testing/testing. htm. The site will link you to your state. Another plus to this site is the information and practice tests about the SAT, ACT, GRE, and more.

As the students take the federal or state mandated tests, note the format. Teachers can do this in the classroom and parents can find the information on the websites. Throughout the school year, use this same format in teacher-made tests or parent-created homework lessons. Incorporate the test direction terminology and commonly used key words for the subject area in the assignments. Use several different types of answer sheets and grids to familiarize the student with the process. Chapter 7 explains more about grids and lists websites to search for printable grids for student use. Primary grade students generally mark their answers directly in the test booklet. Check with the teacher as to whether the students mark answers in the booklet itself or whether they are required to use the grids. The first year the student is exposed to a grid (usually fourth grade) is the time to begin using them often in the classroom.

The materials to use for the lessons are whatever textbooks, trade books, or workbooks the school board has adopted for classroom use. When teaching skills for reading comprehension tests, select passages from the textbooks of the previous grade level or from material used earlier in the school year. When learning a new skill, the student needs to concentrate on that skill alone, thus the purpose of using an independent level of reading material. Once a test-taking skill is mastered, use more difficult material to prepare the student for actual teacher-made tests and those required by the school system. At home, parents can teach these same skills using library books of the student's choice.

See appendix F for a list of key words in the directions and questions that students need to understand. The following list contains directions words that students need to know in order to answer the questions. Remember: do not assume. Elementary students do not have the experience in years to have learned many of these terms.

Bubble in, fill in, darken, mark: All four terms mean the same thing, that is, to indicate with a pencil on a machine-readable form which answer the test taker has chosen.

Compare: Point out the likenesses of the items in question.

Contrast: Point out the differences between the items in question.

Define: Give the meaning, synonym, or book definition of a term.

Describe: Tell the physical characteristics of the item in question.

Estimate: Give an approximate value, generally in math.

Explain: Give reasons, particularly regarding causes, motivation, and so forth.

Illustrate: Give specific examples or draw a diagram or picture.

List: Create a roster of several items that fit into a particular category (e.g., pets: dog, cat, bird, gerbil).

Prove: Show that something is true by giving specific examples.

Read the article/passage/selection/story: Read all the words on the page between the directions and the question. All four words mean the same thing in this context.

State: This direction may also be written as "state the reasons for," and it requires a written response. This direction is not used in tests that are completely scored by a scanner.

Summarize: Briefly state the main points; do not give many details.

Tell about: Write a narrative story about the specific subject.

On all these websites, also look for information that explains how the test is scored, with an explanation of the scoring system. Upon receiving the test results for your child, go to the school for an explanation of anything you do not understand.

A high priority issue for teachers and parents is, "How are these test results going to be used?" The Common Core Standards and accompanying tests were developed as a tool for identifying which students are mastering the grade-level curriculum. Those who are not will not be promoted to the next grade level or class. The states determine which grade levels, which subject areas, and the scores mandatory for promotion. The board of education sites of the state and local school systems are the best choices to locate this information. If not, make personal telephone calls to educators until you get an answer to your questions. Learn this information at the beginning of the school year. These are the questions to ask:

- My child is in ____ grade. What is the criteria for promotion to the next grade?
- Which subject area scores determine promotion?
- What score does my child have to achieve in order to pass?
- Is the test the only criteria for promotion?
- How much weight do the yearly report card grades carry in this decision?
- What are a parent's rights for reviewing and reversing a school system decision?

A common complaint of all this testing was that too much time was spent in the classroom "teaching the test." Teaching the curriculum seemed to be less of a priority. As far back as the 1970s, textbook companies have been creating commercial programs for teaching test-taking skills. Because of the cost, many school systems could not obtain these materials. They were in student workbook form and were an entity unto themselves. A disadvantage to this type of program was that elementary students were not proficient in transferring skills learned in one program to another format—that is, test-taking skills workbooks to actual test.

Much research has been continuing in this area with a common outcome. That is, "teaching the test" is not productive. It is a form of "cramming," and the learning that takes place is very short lasting. Teaching the students "how to take tests" is both more efficient and effective, and the skills will follow the student through the grades. This book was written with that philosophy in mind. It is filled with strategies, techniques, and activities that accomplish this task. The students do not have to transfer information learned in one genre (test-taking skills) into another genre (reading, math, etc.). These students learn the test-taking skills while learning the subject area content. This material has been used in schools with positive results. These results have proven to be a true potential of the student's ability and mastery of the subject.

POINTS TO REMEMBER

- Check the state and school system websites for the following:

  What tests are given?
  Why are the tests given?
  When are the tests given?
  Which subject tests are given in my child's grade?
  What scoring system is used?
  Which tests have a mandated score for promotion?
  How will the teachers and parents be notified of the student's results?
  Who else has access to my child's results?

- Work on the skills as they are taught throughout the school year.
- Cramming just before a test is unproductive.
- Do as many practice tests as you can and from as many different states as possible.
- Young children have a tendency to make this a "life or death" situation. Put the tests in perspective for the child and assure the child of your support, whatever happens.
- There are many groups around the country, educators and parents, who are strongly showing opposition to this law and all it requires. They are looking for changes. That may happen. But the student is required by law to take these tests, so deal in the here and now and support the students as much as possible.

- Learning test-taking skills does not mean the student will "ace" the test. It means the student's score will be an accurate assessment of what that student has learned.

Chapter Three

The Types of Tests and Categories of Test Questions

There are five types of test items that are basic to any test, whether teacher made or commercially made. Every test will not contain all five, but students need to know how to deal with each type. Teachers are familiar with each type of test item, but in this age of accountability, students need to become equally familiar with them. Do not assume that familiarity means mastery. First, teach the formats of the questions on the test. Then, check for understanding and mastery of the process using material from a previous grade level. When selecting or creating test-taking questions, vary the format to give students practice in and familiarity with the performance procedures needed for each type of item.

MULTIPLE CHOICE

This is a test that emphasizes recognition of information. Only information that can be written with one correct answer and three challenging distracters is able to be tested in this format. Items tested are facts, dates, places, and names. Because of the process by which the tests are scored, this format is the predominant choice for test makers. This is the format used in the required state criterion referenced tests. The student marks the answer on a separate answer sheet, which is called a grid. More on the use of grids and where to locate them for practice in your classroom is found in chapter 7. The following are examples of this type of question:

What is the opposite of *up*?

o Several

- ○ Wrong
- ○ Down
- ○ Funny

Jack heard a loud noise. He looked around. It was coming from the woods behind the house. He quickly ran inside. What did he hear?

- ○ A tree
- ○ The TV
- ○ Nothing
- ○ A sound

ALTERNATE RESPONSE

The student taking this type of test chooses between two possible answer choices. The selection comes in the format of true/false, yes/no, right/wrong, or smiley face/frowny face (for early primary). Factual information is tested using this type of question. The following are examples of alternate-response questions:

The opposite of *go* is *stop*.	True	False
The United States is a country.	Right	Wrong
Ice is hot.	Yes	No

MATCHING

In this type of test, students match information in one column to corresponding information in a parallel column. The information tested is primarily recognition of names, dates, numbers, terms, definitions, and specific applications. The following are examples of matching questions:

A. cat	__ a color
B. apple	__ an animal
C. red	__ a flower
D. tulip	__ a fruit

COMPLETION

In a completion question, the test taker is required to fill in the missing word or words in a sentence. This assesses the test taker's ability to recall information and to use context in determining information. This type of question is not usually seen in a computer-scored test. It generally requires a person to decipher the individual handwriting. The following is an example of a completion question. The format would have to be completely reconstructed in order to be scored on a scanner, and in doing so, would make the directions to students very confusing.

Pencil   flew   coat   sailed

1. The boat _____ on the lake.
2. I wrote my spelling words with a _____.
3. Jane wore a _____ to keep warm.
4. The bird _____ over the house.

ESSAY

The student is tested on the ability to use written skills to give information. Expository and narrative formats are used for this purpose. The skills that are tested are logical reasoning, sequencing, expression of ideas, organization of materials, ability to follow directions, and use of English grammar. As concerns about students' writing skills are becoming more prevalent in the twenty-first century, essay tests are used regularly by school systems as benchmark criteria for promotion, graduation, and accountability. School systems using this type of format have created their own test questions and scoring criteria. The creators of the scoring system then train educators selected within their state to manually score them according to a set criteria.

The expository or open-ended format requires the student to respond to a *why* or *how* question. The finished written essay will explain, inform, define, or instruct through facts, examples, and sequential steps. The following are examples of expository essay questions:

1. Everyone has a preferred way in which to spend his or her free time. Think about your favorite hobby or activity. Explain why this is your favorite pastime.
2. A new student enrolls in your school and wants to know the rules of a game played at recess. Think about your favorite game. Write the directions that will explain to the new student how the game is played.

The narrative or on-demand format requires the student to write about something that happened or to write a sequential story on a specific topic. The following are examples of narrative essay questions:

1. Birthdays are special times for everyone. Think about a birthday in your family that you will always remember. Write about what happened on this occasion.
2. When you arrived home from school, a large box was sitting near the front door. Write a story about the box and its contents.

Chapter 21 explains in more detail both the criteria used and the scoring of writing tests. Sample test questions are also listed.

TYPES OF TESTS

A multitude of tests have been created for an equal multitude of subject areas. Some of them are sit-down-paper-and-pencil, some are taken on a computer, some are performance based (actually performing a task that is evaluated by an observer), and for some, the answers are given orally by the test taker to a board of experts in the field. It is all mind-boggling to most folks. This book will only consider those tests that students take in kindergarten through grade twelve.

Criterion Referenced Test: This test was defined, explained, and illustrated in chapter 2. It is the type of test that measures what the students were taught. Priority should be given to teaching the student test-taking skills that relate to the format of these criterion based tests. The No Child Left Behind Act requires states to use the criterion referenced test.

Norm Referenced Test: A norm referenced test is used for comparing one student, or groups of students, with a similar student or group of students. In the case of elementary school students, the norm is generally grade level or age. The students are ranked with other students in their referenced group. The achievement tests that schools used for years were norm referenced tests. They measure general knowledge. For instance, a third-grade student will be ranked nationally with other third-grade students taking the same test. The score is given in percentiles, stanines, or grade level equivalent (see figure 3.1).

- Percentile: A percentile (%ile) is a ranking, not a grade. A grade of 60 percent means the student is failing. The student scored 60 points out of 100 points. A sixtieth percentile means that out of every 100 students, this student scored better than 60 of them and lower than 40 of them. A fiftieth percentile is average.
- Stanine: The stanine is a score on a nine-unit scale from 1 to 9, where a score of 5 describes the average performance. A score of 1, 2, or 3 is considered low. A score of 4, 5, or 6 is average. A score of 7, 8, or 9 are high. The student who scored a sixtieth percentile would have a stanine of

6 and rank in the high average range. This form of scoring was developed by psychologists in World War II for the purpose of testing the military personnel and quickly and conveniently ranking them.

- Grade Equivalent: A grade equivalent indicates the grade level, in years and months. For example, a score of 25 with the grade equivalent of 4.6 means that, on this normed test, 25 was the average score of students in the fourth grade sixth month (September being the first month of school and February being the sixth month). This scoring method is being phased out in favor of percentiles or stanines for it is much more complicated than it seems.
- The percent sign in the top section of the bell curve indicates the percent of national test takers who scored in that range. For example, 20 percent scored in the average or middle range. Four percent scored in the very top range (the geniuses), and another four percent scored in the very bottom range.

Figure 3.1. A Bell Curve: A schematic of the distribution of test scores, showing where in the spectrum the students' scores rank their academic standing (see following page).

Tests Given in Schools

Achievement Test: This test measures the extent to which a student has "achieved" something, acquired certain information, or mastered certain skills. The national achievement tests schools use are for a national population. Thus, what one state may teach at the third-grade level may differ from what another state may teach at the same level. Students in elementary school are taught the same skills, but the sequence of the teaching may vary. These tests are scored in percentiles, stanines, or grade equivalent.

Intelligence Test: This test is also called an aptitude test for it measures abilities. This test measures a student's ability to learn or develop proficiency in a particular area, such as academics, music, numbers, mechanical, etc. The academic intelligence test is given on an individual basis and generally by the school psychologist. These tests require a parent's signature in order to be given to the student.

POINTS TO REMEMBER

- When asked to give permission for your child to be tested, ask what test will be given and why.
- State tests have different scoring criteria. Ask the school personnel to explain their system of scoring.

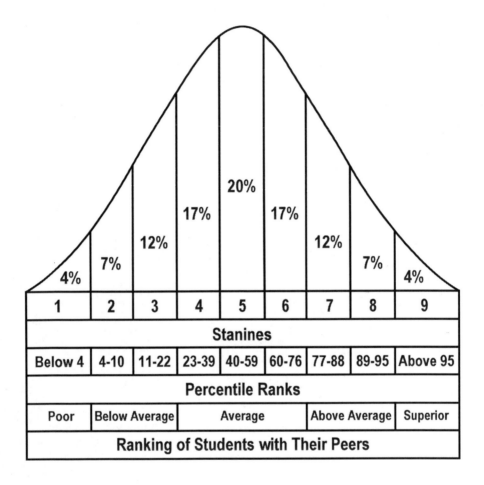

Figure 3.1. Bell Curve

- When the state test scores are sent home to parents, and the information is not clear, call the school and ask for the results to be explained.
- Be aware of the importance of each test and what bearing it has on your child's promotion to the next grade level.
- First, teach the test format, using material from the previous grade level.
- Once format is mastered, use material from the grade level. Elementary students concentrate on one skill at a time.

Chapter Four

Construction of Test Items

SEVEN KEY DEFINITIONS

Should you wish to construct your own tests for your students, you will find it helpful to understand the terms for the parts of the answers and questions. According to the Florida Department of Education *Item Development Workshop* booklet, the definitions are as follows:

1. Key: The correct answer in multiple choice
2. Options: Possible choices for answers in multiple choice
3. Response: Examinee's choice for an answer
4. Stem: The question
5. Stimulus: Material student reacts to in selecting the best answer
6. Distractor: Incorrect answer
7. Foil: Incorrect answer

The question, or stem, must state clearly what is being asked. The correct answer must be clear and unambiguous, and the incorrect choices (distracters) must be both attractive to the examinee who does not know the answer and clearly incorrect to the examinee who does know the answer.

SEVEN WRITING GUIDELINES

When constructing teacher-made or parent-made tests, the following seven guidelines, samples, and examples will help you to ensure that the test items are closely aligned with those found in commercially made tests. These guidelines were presented in the Item Development Workshop conducted by the Florida Department of Education in 1981, in which the author participated. The task at hand was to write test items for the Florida State Student Assessment Test in reading. The writers of these test items were required to follow very specific guidelines of composition. Remember that tests are given to assess information as straightforwardly as possible. They are not intended to trick the student.

1. *The answer choices should contain only one best or correct response.*
   Example:
   Joe saw a white rabbit in the back yard. The rabbit hopped all around the yard. Then it went into a hole near the fence.
   Test Question: Where was the rabbit?
   The following choices are poorly written: two answers could be correct.

   ○ In a box
   ○ In a hole
   ○ In the yard
   ○ At school

   The following choices are better:

   ○ In a box
   ○ In the house
   ○ In the yard
   ○ At school

2. *The grammar must be consistent.*
   Example:
   The elephants walked around the circus ring. Each elephant used its trunk to hold the tail of the elephant in front of it. A pretty girl rode the first elephant. Who rode the elephant?
   The following choices are correctly written; all are nouns.

   ○ A girl
   ○ An elephant
   ○ A boy
   ○ A monkey

   The choices in the following question are correctly written as well; all begin with past-tense verbs.
   The elephants

   ○ Knocked down the tent
   ○ Sat down
   ○ Walked around the ring
   ○ Stood still

The choices in the following question are poorly written. The responses begin with different parts of speech.

What did each elephant hold in its trunk?

○ Moving wagons
○ A tail
○ A log
○ Tightly

3. *Do not give the answer in a previous question or response.*
   Example:
   Bill rode his bike to school. It began to rain. Bill got wet. After he got to school, he called his mom to bring him dry clothes.
   What did Bill ride?

   ○ The school bus
   ○ A bike
   ○ A horse
   ○ A truck

   Where did Bill ride his bike?

   ○ To a park
   ○ In a parade
   ○ To school
   ○ To his house

   The second question is poorly written because it gives the answer to the first question.

4. *Ask one clear question in the simplest language.*
   Example:
   Read the story. Choose the sentence that tells what happened.
   Fred walked through the lunch line. He dropped his tray. There was food all over the floor.

   ○ Fred dropped his tray.
   ○ Fred ate his food.
   ○ Fred mopped up the floor.
   ○ Fred did his homework.

   The first answer is correct. However, the student might think "what happened" to mean "what happened next" and choose the second response.
   The following is another example:
   In our class there are ten boys and twelve girls. Today two students were absent. How many boys and girls were there altogether?

○ 10
○ 12
○ 20
○ 22

This question is poorly written. Is it asking how many boys and girls are usually in the class or how many are in the class today?

5. *Put as much wording as possible in the question, but only the facts.*
   Example:
   Mother and Sally went shopping. They bought some red shoes. Sally wore the new shoes home. What did they buy?

   ○ They bought some shoes.
   ○ They bought some candy.
   ○ They bought a dog.
   ○ They bought some socks.

   The answer choices should be written in simplest form: shoes, candy, a dog, and socks. Unnecessary wording is confusing to students.

6. *Put no irrelevant material in the stem or the response.*
   Example:
   My new shirt has stars on the front. Count the stars.

   *   *   *   *   *

   ○ 2
   ○ 5
   ○ 9
   ○ 11

   This is a math problem, not reading. "My new shirt has stars on the front" is irrelevant.

7. *Vary the position of the responses. Do not put the answers in a pattern.*
   The following arrangement is not good: 1. A, 2. B, 3. C, 4. A, 5. B, 6. C, 7. A, 8. B, 9. C.
   A random arrangement of answers, such as 1. A, 2. C, 3. A, 4. B, 5. C, 6. A, 7. C, 8. B, 9. B is better.
   As a homework assignment (grades four and up), allow students to create a test item. They will develop a clearer understanding of the test format.

POINTS TO REMEMBER

- Use material from the grade-level reading and social studies textbooks in writing test questions.
- Assign students the task of writing test questions with four answer choices using the same material.
- Use practice test questions from other state tests in teaching this skill.
- Always critique each answer as to which is correct and why, as well as which are wrong and why.

Chapter Five

Weekly Format and Lesson Plans

Select the skill of the week, for example, main idea, sequence, or cause and effect. Then select material (preferably previously learned) from the classroom textbooks that you will use to teach the skill. The skill or skills will remain the same all week. Students may take two to three weeks to achieve mastery of the more complex test-taking skills.

Appendix D contains a suggested weekly plan format, and appendix E contains a sample daily lesson plan form. Create a similar format for the teaching assignment that meets the needs of the students. A sample lesson plan for a week is provided at the end of this chapter.

MONDAY

While the students are reading the passage, write the questions and four answer choices on the marker board, on an overhead projector, or in a Power-Point program. Putting the sample questions on a transparency or saving them in your computer will allow them to be shared with other teachers and saved for use in subsequent years.

The questions must be written in test format—that is, with each question having four answer choices. Remember to put a bubble in front of or underneath each answer choice.

After they read the passage and the questions, the students should jot their answers on paper. Discuss the question with students, and identify the correct response by pinpointing the facts in the passage. Then discuss the three incorrect choices, and, again, identify why they are incorrect by locating the material in the passage or noting material that is not in the passage. See chapters 10 to 12 for more detailed strategies in choosing the correct answer for multiple choice questions.

Examples:

1. The main idea of the story is:

     A. (An answer completely off target)
     B. (The main idea of one page or paragraph, but not of the entire
         passage)
     C. (A statement about one unimportant fact in the selection)
     D. (The correct answer)

2. The (effect) happened because (cause).

     A. (A factual statement about a previous story)
     B. (A statement about the effect)
     C. (The correct answer)
     D. (A statement about the cause, but not the cause itself)

Remember to vary the position of the correct answer.

TUESDAY

Repeat the format of Monday's lesson, using a different selection from your
reading or social studies textbook.

WEDNESDAY AND THURSDAY

Repeat the same format of Monday's and Tuesday's lessons, but guide students toward selecting the correct and incorrect responses and documenting
their choices. As a homework assignment or classroom practice activity,
assign each student specific pages of the material being worked on in class.
The students, in grades four and above, will read the pages and then write
one test question with four answer choices. This is graded as any other
homework assignment. You will later use some of these as actual questions
on the teacher-made test.

FRIDAY

Assign students the material to read. Use your preferred method of presentation to display two test questions. The students will answer the questions
independently on paper and turn in their responses to you with no discussion
about response choices. The grade will not be recorded in the grade book, but
will indicate to the students and teacher whether or not the material is being
mastered. Discuss the correct answers after you have checked the papers and

handed them back to the students. Use the practice bubble sheets (grid) that you have printed out from the Internet sources (found at the end of chapter 7). These grids usually have capabilities for recording answers to about fifty questions, thus it may be used for several lessons.

Once the students know that the scores on the tests will not be recorded in the grade book, their test anxiety will be alleviated and they will concentrate on learning the test-taking skill. Emphasize to the students that these test questions are important learning experiences, not just another graded paper.

SAMPLE WEEKLY LESSON PLAN

The following is an example of a week's lessons. For your purposes, select a passage from the students' textbook. Your task is then to write one or two test items for each day's activity. Writing these activities can be time consuming. By sharing the task with teammates on the grade level, each teacher only has a portion of the work and the lessons reach many more students.

For example, the test directions would tell students to read the following passage:

"Did you know that chocolate grows on trees? Over two thousand years ago, the cacao (pronounced kah-KOW) tree was discovered in the rainforests in the Americas. Chocolate is made from the seeds that grow in the pods on cacao trees.

"The ancient Mexicans were the first people known to make chocolate. They ground up the seeds and made a tasty drink. In the early 1500s, the Spanish explorers came to Mexico and tasted the drink. They liked it very much. They took some seeds back to Spain.

"Within one hundred years, the chocolate drink became a favorite all over Europe. In fact, some German people made a machine to make chocolate candy. They took this machine to the United States in 1893 to show at the Chicago World's Fair.

"A young man named Milton Hershey saw the machine, liked the chocolate, and bought one of the machines. He brought the machine to his hometown in Darry Church, Pennsylvania. In 1905, he opened the Hershey Chocolate Manufacturing Plant and made chocolate candy. It is now the largest chocolate candy plant in the world."

Monday's Lesson

What is the best title for this story?

- o The Uses of Chocolate
- o The Discovery of Chocolate Seeds
- o The Story of the Cacao Tree

    o The History of Chocolate

Tuesday's Lesson

What is the main idea for the last paragraph?

    o Milton Hershey liked chocolate.
    o Chocolate comes to the United States.
    o Darry Church is in Pennsylvania.
    o The Hershey bar is one hundred years old.

Wednesday's Lesson

What is the main idea of the story?

    o All about ancient Mexicans
    o All about chocolate
    o All about Milton Hershey
    o All about the chocolate machine

Thursday's Lesson

Select another passage from the textbook and ask, "What is the main idea of the passage?" or "What is the best title for the passage?"

Friday's Lesson

Select yet a different passage from the textbook and ask the same questions. The students select the most appropriate response from the four answer choices that you have written.

    When students write book reports, include in the requirements a sentence stating the main idea of the book, and also, require the student to create a new title for the book.

POINTS TO REMEMBER

- Identifying why three answers are incorrect is just as important as identifying why one is correct.
- When first teaching the skill, use material from a previous grade level.
- After the skill is mastered, use grade-level material.
- Use material from all genres in the curriculum.
- Teach one skill a week in collaboration with a specific subject area.

Chapter Six

Techniques: The Anxiety Factor

At the beginning of this book, the three factors that have a bearing on how successful a student is on a test were stated: 1) knowledge of the material, 2) test anxiety, and 3) test-taking skills (test-wiseness). Teachers in this nation do a better-than-satisfactory job in teaching the basic skills. By also teaching the students test-taking strategies, they will help their students become familiar with the test format. In turn, this takes away some of the stress that causes the test anxiety. The students then give their full focus to the test and ultimately obtain a score that is a true measure of their potential.

Before anxiety can be dealt with, it must be understood what it is and how it affects a person, physically and psychologically. Anxiety has been studied since the early 1950s. Anxiety is a predicament or condition in which the person is uncomfortable, apprehensive, or fearful about something that may happen. In the testing situation, the fear is generally that of failing and what may result because of it. In psychiatry, this is an abnormal state in which the person, or test takers in this case, feels powerless and unable to cope with what they perceive as a threatening situation. Although the outcome the test taker envisions may be imaginary, the emotional and physical factors experienced by the student are a reality.

Taking a test in which the student has knowledge of the material, but the test format is completely foreign is a prime reason for anxiety and poor test scores. For example, scores on the spelling portion of the standardized test are not indicative of the student's spelling skills. Rather, they are an indication of the student's understanding of the test format. On a classroom spelling test, the teacher says the word and the students write it on their paper. On a standardized spelling test, not only is the format different, but also the cognitive skill involved is more complex. In each case, the teacher's directions are the same.

However, instead of writing the word, the student has to select the correctly spelled word from among four words. For many test takers, this type of format is very confusing and leads to low scores. Elementary school students, particularly in the primary grades, cannot always make the transition from giving out information (spelling the word on paper) to selecting from information given to them (choosing the correct word from among four that look very similar to each other).

This is easily remedied by teaching the student the skills in the same format he or she will encounter on the test. Teachers can view the test and make notes of format in all subject areas. Parents can view tests on the state's websites and note the format. This is not "teaching the test." The test items will be written in the test format, but the material used will come from classroom textbooks. This is done throughout the school year.

Possible reasons for the anxiety expressed by elementary and high school students are:

- My performance won't please my parents, my teacher, or my friends.
- I won't pass my class or grade level.
- I won't get accepted into the college I want.
- I won't qualify for the college scholarship.
- I feel dumb!
- I didn't study enough and knew I wasn't ready.
- I felt as if the world was on my shoulders.

These last three reasons were expressed the most, and the students truly believed that was the outcome they had to look forward to:

- If I do poorly, my parents won't love me anymore.
- My whole future depends on this test.
- What will happen to me if I don't do well?

This is the list of the physical effects most observed in the test takers:

- Palms perspire or hands grow cold
- Breathing or heartbeat quickens
- Stomach gets queasy and may result in vomiting
- Cramps
- Faintness or dizziness
- Headache
- Muscles grow tense
- Lack of sleep or too much sleep
- Loss of or increased appetite
- Tears before, during, or after the test

- Memory fails and the students are sure they forgot everything they ever learned

In a stressful situation, the body actually concentrates the blood supply into its central cavity instead of its extremities. Thus, the physical symptoms. These responses put our body on alert. In some cases, this can actually help increase performance. The phrase "that person's adrenalin just kicked in!" may be a truism. The physical symptoms may be evident even days before the test.

Test anxiety can affect students by:

- Increasing their levels of stress
- Causing or reinforcing negative attitudes toward self, subject area, schooling, or testing
- Prompting students to cheat on tests
- Decreasing levels of motivation
- Depressing levels of test performance
- Contributing to greater levels of test anxiety [1]

Test-taking anxiety has been the subject of research studies by educators, psychiatrists, and psychologists for over sixty years. In this author's own research study, the students in an elementary school (one of thirty-nine in the school district) raised their ranking in the school district. They had consistently scored in the 4th quartile on the national achievement tests. After being taught test-taking skills, they raised their ranking to the 3rd quartile. Teachers noted an improvement in positive behavior, especially with the absence of tears. [2]

However, knowledge of test-taking skills will alleviate only some of the anxiety. The next step is to learn coping skills to deal with the emotions of test taking. Beginning as early as first grade, students need to be taught that tests are just one tool in assessing their achievement or mastery of a subject. Tests are to be respected, not feared.

With the state criterion referenced tests, the student's score on that one test may result in not being promoted. The SAT, ACT, or GRE results in a one time score that determines acceptance into a college or qualifying for a scholarship. In most cases, there are "second chances" for a make-up or another try at the test. The tests and what scores the student earns are to be put into perspective. Support from parents and teachers is needed both before and after the test. If all does not go well, have a "Plan B" ready that will give the student a different direction. Above all, give the student a sense of worth and discuss how to deal with an unpleasant and unfortunate situation. Emphasize the student's effort over achievement.

Elementary students can be quite resourceful when learning to cope with unpleasant situations. The following are actual comments told to classroom teachers when asked how the student handled the anxiety:

- Self! You can do this! (fourth-grade girl)
- Stop the bad thoughts. They rot the brain! (sixth-grade boy)
- I think I can. I think I can. I think I can. (third-grade boy whose favorite book was *The Little Engine That Could*)
- I can do this. I'm a smart dude! (fifth-grade boy)
- Hey brain! Get a move on. I need some help here! (fifth-grade girl)

As you can see, they can also be quite creative and have a sense of humor.

A survey was given to the fifth-grade students in a large elementary school about two weeks before the "big tests." Here are some of the questions and responses:

- *I would do better on tests if I* _____ . Most of the answers were related to work and study habits, for example:

    Read the book
    Listened to the teacher
    Studied harder
    Did my homework
    Did my classwork
    Paid attention

- *I do poorly on tests because I* _____. The responses were overwhelmingly "don'ts" and were repetitious of the previous answers.
- *When I take a test, I feel* _____ *because* _____. Most answers as to how the students felt were some sort of anxiety. The "because" answers were in two opposite realms: one from the "A" students who were afraid they would not maintain their A grades, and the other from the poor students who were afraid they would not pass. There were also many students who stated they were worried that their parents would not love them if they did not do well.
- Approximately 34% of the students said they experienced the physical symptoms and worried about the results. They weren't sure what the word anxiety meant, but their descriptions of their feelings when taking tests were accurate definitions.

One of the first steps in alleviating anxiety is to discuss with students the reason tests are given and the many uses for them. At the beginning of the school year, make a chart of these reasons. Examples include the following:

    To pass to the next grade

To provide accountability for the teacher, school, and school district
For the teacher to know that the student knows the material
For report card grades
To qualify for special programs (gifted, special education)
To get a driver's license
To get into college and professional schools
To qualify for college scholarships
To be accepted into the military
To get a professional license
To get a job or a job promotion

Knowing about the test, the format, and procedures helps place the students in their comfort zone, not in anxiety mode. Avail yourself of the website and school personnel to learn all you can about the tests:

- When will the student get the results?
- How will the student get the results?
- Who else will get the results?
- How will the results be used?
- What is the format for the results (percentile, stanine, grade equivalent)?
- When and where will the test be given (as in ACT, SAT, GRE)?
- What materials will you need (paper, pencils, eraser, pens)?
- What is required for entrance to SAT, ACT, GRE (identification, pre-printed registration form/money and remember directions and times)?
- Will there be a particular seating arrangement?
- How will make-ups be done, if allowed?
- Will the test be timed?
- Will the administrator or teacher explain procedures and answer questions before the test?
- What help may be given during the test?
- What should the student do when finished before time is up?
- What if the pencil breaks?
- Do I get a bathroom break?

Sitting in a wooden or metal chair for a length of time can become uncomfortable, especially in a stressful testing situation. This is true regardless of the student's learning style. Students are not allowed to stand up and stretch or walk off the kinks in the body. This is especially difficult for young children. Teach your student these two muscle relaxers to ease the stress. Remember to wear loose-fitting and comfortable clothing.

- While sitting erect in the chair, lift the legs straight up under the desk so they are perpendicular to the body. Stretch the legs out as far as possible

while still sitting erect in the chair. Slowly put the legs back down so the feet are touching the floor. Repeat this five or six times.
• While sitting erect in the chair, put your arms straight down the sides of your body. Make fists of your hands. Then open the hands and stretch the fingers as much as possible. Do this five or six times.

These two exercises will take just a few minutes, will not disturb the other test takers in the room, and will ease the stress. Sometimes just a short break in the task will give the person a boost in energy and motivation.

What can the student do to deal with the anxiety?

The do nots:

• Do not worry about "What if . . ."
• Do not "should" on yourself:
I should have studied more.
I should have paid attention in class.
I shouldn't have spent so much time texting or in social media sites.
I should have eaten a better breakfast, or I should have eaten less breakfast.
I should have gotten more or less sleep.
I shouldn't have paid so much attention to what the other students are doing.

The dos:

• *Follow the guidelines of test-taking skills.*
• Maintain a positive attitude.
• Repeat (to yourself) your own motivational phrase (e.g., Take this test! Don't let it take you!).
• Expect the best of yourself and "give it all you've got."
• Go into the test situation prepared (materials and "gear").
• Remember that stress and your reaction to it are natural. Use it as a motivation to do well.
• For test situations, such as the SAT, ACT, or GRE, arrive at the test site early so you can get a "good seat":

Do not sit near the window or the wall adjacent to a hallway. Both situations may result in distracting noise. Right-brained students may thrive in sitting in either place.
Do not sit near your friends. Separate so you can each concentrate on the test.
Dress for the weather. Forget style; wear clothing that is comfortable.

As you walk into the testing room, push the weight of the world off your shoulders (actually use your hand to brush off your shoulders; it will give you a laugh and relax the tension).

- For students taking the state required criterion referenced tests, take as many practice tests on the state websites as possible. It will acquaint you with the format and relieve some tension.
- For students taking the SAT, ACT, or other qualifying tests, take them as early as the sophomore or beginning of the junior year in high school. Your score will be ranked with your peers so you will get an idea of where you stand in the scheme of things. Do not worry about the score. Pay attention to the format, timed portions, type of questions, and subject matter. The next time you take it, you will be more relaxed and knowledgeable of the test. The knowledge and confidence will result in an improved score.

The rest of this chapter is composed of several activities that help put students in tune with their feelings about tests and put test taking into a more positive perspective for them. These activities may be done in a classroom or at home. The student may enjoy inviting a few friends to the house to take part in this "preparing for the tests" activity.

ACTIVITIES

Activity 1

Give each student a sticky note, and tell them to write one feeling they have had when hearing the word *test*. Each student then says the word and sticks the note on a chart under one of three headings: emotional, physical, or academic. As the students see that their responses mirror their peers' responses, they will feel more free to have a discussion on the subject. There are two rules for this activity: 1) all ideas are worthy, and 2) put-downs are not allowed.

Activity 2

Survey the students with the following questions, adding some of your own. This will also develop into a healthy discussion. Students will be surprised that it is okay to not like tests and it is okay to say so.

1. I would do better on tests if _____.
2. When I take a test, I feel _____ because _____.
3. To get over this feeling, I _____.

4. The worst thing I remember about a test is _____.
5. The best thing I remember about a test is _____.
6. I did my best when _____.
7. I did my poorest when _____.
8. When I take a test, I tell myself _____.

Activity 3

The students will use the survey questions listed in activity 2 to interview three people. One person has to be a parent, one has to be a peer, and the other is the student's choice. The students like to interview the school principal or the coach for this activity. The students will share their responses in an oral class activity. The object is to bring to the students' attention the fact that many others have the same feelings about taking tests. Parents may also assign this lesson and then have a family discussion.

Activity 4

Have students write a letter to the school principal, their state or federal representatives (they are making many of the laws requiring testing), or the school superintendent stating their opinion about tests and why or why not to eliminate or curtail them from the school district's curriculum.

Activity 5

Make a chart using the words from all the surveys in activity 2 concerning the feelings about tests. Discuss why people might have those feelings, and then list ways to alleviate them.

Activity 6

Have the students write a poem about tests, possibly in limerick format.

Activity 7

Have students write a letter to the editor of the local newspaper expressing their opinions about tests and relating how elementary school students feel about them.

Activity 8

Have students write a story: "How I Sent the Test-Taking Worries into Space!"

Activity 9

Have the class work together to compose a letter to the publisher of the school's standardized test. Have students tell the good things about their test as well as the bad things, and tell them how the publisher can make the test better for the students. Also have students ask them how tests are made. A representative of the publisher may even visit the class.

POINTS TO REMEMBER

- *YOU CAN IF YOU THINK YOU CAN!*

Chapter Seven

Techniques: Format Familiarity

When updating a test-preparation program, a teacher piloted the technical aspects with the fourth graders in her classroom. She gave each student a blank bubble sheet (grid) for the lesson. She then reminded them about the format of the third-grade tests, in which they bubbled in their answers in a consumable test booklet. The students' groans and body language told her of their opinions of those tests.

However, she went on to explain that the procedure was different for fourth grade. Instead of marking in their booklets, they would use a separate answer sheet, called a grid, similar to the ones they had on their desks. Then she informed them of why it was important for them to learn this procedure. Throughout the school year, they would practice using the bubble sheets to become comfortable with the format by test-taking time. They would also be using this type of answer sheet for classroom tests.

For practice, the students were told to bubble in the space (oval or circle) of the numbers as the teacher called them out. She began calling the numbers: 2. C, 4. A, 7. B. The reaction of the students completely surprised her. Many frantically waved their hands in the air, and some even yelled, "Wait!" Some students looked around the room to see the reactions of their classmates, and others just sat there with blank looks on their faces. The teacher got the message and stopped the lesson. This format was even more foreign to them than had been anticipated.

The next twenty minutes were spent exploring the bubble sheet, including a thorough explanation of every aspect of the grid. The class talked about the purpose of the sheet, the reason for the change to this format, and when they would be expected to use it. At this point, the teacher shared her findings with the other teachers on her grade level as well as the fifth- and sixth-grade teachers in the school.

The school test coordinator gave these teachers three different types of blank grids to use with their students throughout the school year. After the state achievement tests were given in the spring, the teachers shared their experiences and the outcome at a faculty meeting. The frustration experienced by both teachers and students in previous years was no longer a factor in the test results.

Before folks learn how to drive a car, they first need to become familiar with the technical aspects of the vehicle: how to turn everything off and on, where to put gas into the car, and the purpose of every pedal and instrument. The same is true for students taking tests. Becoming familiar with the test format, or the technical aspects of the tests, will help alleviate test anxiety. Do not skip this lesson. Remember, there will still be a bell curve (see chapter 3) of test scores in your classroom after students have learned test-taking skills, but students' scores will be a more accurate assessment of their potential. These skills will also help students do as well as they are able on written tests they will take for college entrance exams, scholarship qualification, licenses, and jobs in the future.

The beginning of the school year is the time for testing techniques to be introduced. Then the skills will need to be reinforced before every test given in the class. Remember: do not assume. Review and reteach test-taking skills every school year, integrating it in the school curriculum.

UNDERSTANDING THE TEST ITSELF

Ask the school curriculum specialist or county-level person to supply you with the following information on the important standardized tests, or at least get the information a few weeks before each test date. Explain and emphasize the following points about the test:

- What kind of test is being given? (state mandated criterion referenced test, norm referenced achievement, assessment, reading, math, or other subject area tests)
- Why is the test being given? (the criteria for promotion, mastery of chapter or book material, placement into a special program, general information, report card grade, or passing/failing)
- What type of items are on the test? (essay, matching, completion, multiple choice, or true/false)
- What will the grade be used for? (pass/fail, subject grades for a report card, or ranking of school in district)
- Who will get the results? (student, teacher, parent, principal, other school system personnel, school system website, or the media)

MATERIALS NEEDED FOR TESTING

Students need to know at the beginning of the school year the materials required at every testing session: two number-two pencils with dull points, one number-two pencil for writing words, and a good eraser.

Children will sharpen their pencils to the sharpest point possible; however, insist on and demonstrate why a dull point is better. First, a sharp point will break easily under the pressure of bubbling in, causing frustration. Second, the dull point is wider and will bubble in each space at a faster rate, thus saving precious time.

BUBBLING IN

Students should be taught to always bubble spaces in from the center out, as shown in the following examples. Scoring machines scan the center of the space when checking the answer.

Figure 7.1. Correct and incorrect ways to bubble in

Many elementary children are meticulous in bubbling in the spaces on their answer sheets and thereby waste time on timed tests. Once the proper bubbling method is innate, students will mark their answers more quickly and move on to the next question. Students should also be taught to erase all other pencil marks, for the scoring machine cannot tell the difference between a stray mark and the correct answer. Provide pencils with dull points for students to use when giving classroom or home school tests.

ACTIVITY

Allow the students to become familiar with machine-readable answer sheets before they are used for tests. Because kindergarten through third-grade students mark their answers for standardized tests in the test booklet, this activity is used for fourth grade and above.

Give each child a blank answer sheet. Call letters and numbers (e.g., 1. A, 4. C) and tell the students to mark the corresponding space on their answer sheet. When the activity is completed, the darkened spaces will represent a picture or symbol, for example, the number 4, a dollar sign, or a sailboat. Ask the students to guess what picture is formed. For additional practice, allow the students to create their own pictures.

Acquisition of grids for classroom practice:

- Contact school- or county-level testing coordinator for a copy.
- In your favorite search engine, type in: "sample test-taking bubble sheets." There are several site choices.
- Iowa State University provides several printable versions, your choice of black, blue, or green: www.it.iastate.edu/services/tes/sheets. This form has half grid and half student identification information. Many school test grids come preprinted with the student information. Teach the skill of filling in the student information as they will encounter it in the higher grades.
- This site is for the creative teacher or parent: www.catpin.com/bubbletest. The site gives step-by-step directions on how to create a grid that meets your exact needs. The creator selects the number of answers, the size and color, and much, much more.

POINTS TO REMEMBER

- Bring three number-two pencils (two blunt points for bubbling in, one sharp point for writing student information) and an eraser (a separate eraser—not at the end of the pencil).
- Erase mistakes completely and carefully.
- Bubbling in: The scanner picks up the center of the circle (any shape). Start bubbling in from the center out and completely fill in the space.
- Match the number of the question to the number on the grid.
- When you skip a question you do not know, also skip the same number on the answer sheet.
- Identify key words in the question first. Then read every answer and select the option that matches the key words.
- NEVER GIVE UP! A quitter never wins. (Or select another adage that is meaningful to the student and will be a motivational force during the test.)

Chapter Eight

Styles of Learning

At a country music awards ceremony, the female singer-of-the-year held her trophy close to her body and, teary-eyed, began her list of "thank-yous." She concluded her heartfelt speech with a special "thank you" to her husband. She stated that she could not have accomplished all she did without his help. She said, "I am the thinker-upper and he is the doer."

Their learning styles were opposites, but they complemented each other and the outcome was a very successful team.

A learning style is the way in which we learn. It is how we respond to the environment and process the information. There are two factors to consider.

The first is whether a person is predominantly a left-brained or a right-brained learner. The left brain is the "academic" side with sequence, reasoning, logic, and organization. The right brain is the "creative" side with rhythm, movement, face recognition, and imagination. Neither is better; they are just different.

The other factor is that of modalities: vision (seeing), auditory (hearing), or tactile/kinesthetic (touching or doing). There is no right way or wrong way in which to learn.

We learn best in the ways that are inherent to us. The explanation here is to give the teacher or parent enough information to recognize the learning style of the student. To learn more in depth, go to your favorite search engine and type in:

- Left brain/right brain
- Learning styles
- Learning modalities

LEFT BRAIN/RIGHT BRAIN

In the late 1960s and early 1970s, research was begun that completely changed our conception of the brain and what its purpose is in our learning. It was discovered that there are two sides to the brain and that they are linked by a very complex network of nerve fibers. Previously, the brain was thought to be one complete lobe. [1]

The following chart outlines the basic characteristics of a left-brained or right-brained person. Remember, one side predominates, but the other side is in play also. The degree of the dominance is also different in each person.

Left-Brained	**Right-Brained**
1. Analytical: Starts at the beginning and plans the step-by-step process to completion	1. Global: Sees the bottom line and then decides what steps are needed to get there
2. Everything in sequence: makes lists, schedules, agendas, outlines	2. Random processing: moves (flits) from one task to another (even if not finished)
3. Logical	3. Emotional, dramatic
4. Plans ahead	4. Impulsive
5. Studying: Quiet, organization of materials, formal setting with good light	5. Studying: Has to have noise, television, or music; gets what is needed, when needed; any setting is fine, needs comfort
6. Sees differences	6. Sees likenesses
7. Speaks with few gestures	7. Body movement when speaking
8. Verbal: Likes reading, words language; mathematicians	8. Visual: creative; music, dance, art, athletes

First, recognize your own style of learning. Then recognize the student and gear the teaching to the style of learning required for mastery of skills by that student. A right-brained child may not be being disrespectful when accepting a cluttered bedroom. Organization is not that child's forte. A left-brained child may seem to annoy the adult with constant lists on the hand-held device. Lists are a way of life to that child. Teach to the child's strengths. Then teach the student how to use the strengths to offset the weaknesses.

MODALITIES

A modality is a style of learning in which students use their senses. As with left-brain/right-brain learning, one is usually predominant but the others all are used when needed. They also may be used either independently or in correlation with each other. The senses are seeing, hearing, and touching/movement.

A typical classroom contains about 25% to 30% visual, 25% to 30% auditory, 15% tactile/kinesthetic, and 25% to 30% mixed.[2]

The traits of each are:

1. *Visual (seeing):* This learner prefers anything visual—that is, print material, diagrams, charts, graphs, tables, pictures, and PowerPoint presentations. A lecture needs to be accompanied by visuals in order for this learner to remember the presentation. They remember things they can see in their minds. The learner tends to be left-brained: organized, language skills, neat, quite study setting, and detail oriented.
2. *Auditory (hearing):* This learner learns best by listening to speeches, lectures, tapes, television (doesn't need to watch), or conversations with others. To enjoy and comprehend reading, this learner needs to read out loud or be read to. The learner enjoys lectures, panel or class discussions, and conversations. This learner is more likely to be right-brained and likes music, even when studying. This person is able to function well in an unorganized setting, be it people or things.
3. *Tactile (touching)/kinesthetic (movement):* This learner cannot sit still for very long and needs to be moving. This style of learning is found in musicians, athletes, dancers, actors, building contractors, and any profession that requires physical activity and movement. This person tends to be messy, tolerates clutter, is quite outgoing, likes to doodle, and is willing to try new things. The learner is also more likely to be right-brained and very creative (artists in all dimensions).

Students who are not performing well have been told, "You are smart and could do this if you would just try harder" or "focus" or "concentrate." Students want to do well. The reason the students do not perform well is not usually a lack of intelligence. The student is not being taught to his or her innate strengths. When working with the child, first identify the strengths and then teach the student through the strengths. Use the strengths to teach the student how to compensate for the weaknesses.

The first factor in determining success on a test is knowledge of the material (see chapter 1). This includes what is learned in the school setting as well as what is learned through homework assignments. At the beginning of the school year, set up a study center at home for school assignments and projects. This is a year-long process for each grade level. Use the student's learning styles to create this area. It does not have to be elaborate or have all the latest equipment, furniture, or supplies. It *does* have to be effective for the appropriate style of learning. Allow the student to collaborate on the project. If the area has to be shared, make it a team effort. Schedules and rules may have to be established for it to work effectively and efficiently. Once agreed upon, have the students type the information on their hand-held devices or laptop. Then print it out and post it in the designated area.

The third factor in determining success in taking tests is test-wiseness. When selecting the activities from this book in teaching the skills, carefully choose those that meet the criteria for the student's style of learning.

THE ROLE OF TECHNOLOGY

One section of the No Child Left Behind Act of 2000 was concerned with the role of technology in education. With the influx of technology in the classroom and in our personal lives came the change in the role of the teacher and the student.

Teachers were the lecturer, the presenter, the authority of the data. Textbooks were the required form of what information was taught and how it was dispensed. Students were the passive recipients of the information.

In the age of technology, teachers are now facilitators, mentors, guides, and tutors. They now teach the students "how to learn." Students are now active in their learning. They are taught how to access the information, assess its value, analyze the authenticity of it, and arrive at a conclusion of what meets their needs in the scheme of information at the time. The teaching process may have changed, but the learning process remains the same. The student learns best through his or her inborn style of learning.

Long gone are the passive students who parrot facts, rote learn, and memorize data. Critical thinking is at the forefront. The new state tests reflect this skill in their style of questioning. Students like immediate results, and technology fulfills that need. Technology and the active roles both teachers and students take in the process increase motivation.

In 1986-1987, the District of Columbia public schools carried on a research project in their inner-city schools. This study validated that students who were taught *how to learn* learned for a lifetime. The initial group was preschoolers, and the study followed these students through fourth grade.[3] The students were divided into three groups:

- Child-initiated classrooms: These students selected the focus of their learning. Without realizing what they were doing, the students used their style of learning in which to learn. At the end of the preschool year, these students had learned more basic skills than either of the other groups.

- Academically directed classrooms: These classrooms had teacher-directed activities in which the students had no choice as to the activities. As they progressed through first and second grade, the social skills of these students declined as well as some academic skills.
- Middle-of-the-road classrooms: These classrooms combined the philosophies of both the other classrooms. The students in this setting were significantly behind the other students at the end of the preschool year.

By fourth grade, the students in the child-initiated classroom were academically more advanced than the others. They had learned through their innate learning styles as well as performed in an atmosphere that was conducive to their age-appropriate development. This system taught them how to learn and strengthened their critical thinking skills.

By fourth grade, the students in the academic group, who had learned to follow precise and exact directions, could not perform without being told specifically what to do and how to do it. The students in the child-centered group were told, "You are here at point A and you need to get to point B." They did. If one strategy did not work, they tried another and another until they accomplished the task.

This research, as well as that of left-brain/right-brain and learning modalities, has required educators to change both their philosophy as well as techniques in teaching. Students need strong critical thinking skills that enable them to work independently and be self-reliant to choose options available to them through technology. These are exciting times.

Relating Test-Taking Skills to the Student's Style of Learning

The learning style of a student determines the test taker's performance on the results of the standardized test.

The person who is predominantly left brained concentrates on information and data. This information and data is based on logic and sequence: material that has been, is being, or can be proven. The left-brained student deals in facts, everything being black and white, no gray areas.

The student is comfortable in the testing situation: a paper and pencil format that is predominantly reading. The student understands the process and works logically and sequentially through the test, starting at number 1 and working through to the last question. First the directions are read (probably twice). Then the question is read, with emphasis on key words, each answer choice is considered, and the answer grid is marked accordingly.

The person who is right brained has a much more difficult time with the format. This person also deals with information and data. However, this information and data are based, not on proof, but on what is perceived or experienced. The predominantly reading format is foreign and frustrating for this student. This student thrives on any graphics that are in the test. Fortunately for this test taker, technology is responsible for many more types of graphics in the criterion referenced tests. Students are not only expected to read words, but also to "read" many charts, graphs, tables, and diagrams.

There are techniques and strategies that are helpful to both types of learners. The modality preference of the student is also considered.

- The first step is to teach the student to read and process the information in the directions. The skill has to be taught to all students in all formats.
- Give the directions orally. When first teaching the skill, read every direction. After the students have selected their best performance option for this skill, discontinue reading every direction and read only what is stipulated in the test giver's manual.
- Tell the student to read the directions out loud.
- Tell the student to read the directions by saying each word, mouthing them, not out loud.
- Tell the student to read the directions silently.
- Tell the student to mouth the words in the directions as the student finger points to each word.

    After a period of time, the student will select the method that corresponds with the predominant learning style. At that time, remind students that in a testing situation, nothing can be spoken out loud. This process will put the students in their own comfort zone, thus lessening test-taking anxiety.

- A left-brained person starts at the beginning of a task and works methodically through to the end or a finished product. The right-brained person visualizes the finished product and then decides the steps needed to accomplish the task, sometimes in random order. Teach both ways. Start with very short classroom tests of no more than ten items. Work together methodically completing each item from 1 through 10. Use this method several times. Then, again using another short test, work from 10 back to 1, stressing with each item to match the number of the question to the number on the answer grid. Lead the students to the conclusion that the completed test shows answers, not the order in which the questions were done. Another technique in this process is to skip a question and come back to it after all other questions are answered. Stress again to make sure the number of the question matches the number on the answer grid. Students will gravitate to the method that matches their own style of learning and be comfortable with the process.

- Another activity is to use a math lesson similar to the example in chapter 16. Use this example to teach the students to look over the test first before deciding where to begin. Look at the first five questions and the last five questions. If the questions increase in difficulty as the student progresses toward the end, always start with number one. The student will complete more questions and have more correct answers.
- The left-brained person looks at the differences. The right-brained person looks at the similarities. Teach both ways and stress that the student may choose either method. The practice tests on the state websites offer lessons already planned. Print out the test questions. Allow students time to complete them, usually only eight to ten questions. Then use the material containing the answers to answer why one is correct and the others are incorrect. This process will speak to both learning styles. The students will ultimately select the process that is compatible with their learning style.

POINTS TO REMEMBER

- If a child does not respond to directions given in one format, try a different format.
- The student is more successful when teacher and parent share this information and work together in support of the student.
- After you have identified the student's style of learning, research it more thoroughly on the Internet.
- The student who learns how to learn through the innate learning styles will be prepared for the new tests that require critical thinking skills and the ability to "read" graphics to get information.
- There are many sources on the Internet listing activities for elementary students.
- Be flexible. It is difficult teaching and working with a child who has a different learning style than your own.
- The more times a student hears a direction (e.g., match the number of the question to the number on the answer grid), the higher the probability that student will remember it during the test.

Chapter Nine

Following Directions

A first-grade teacher carefully read the directions of the math computation portion of the yearly standardized test to her first-grade students. This was her first year as a teacher, and she wanted to be sure that she did everything right. As the students began their work, she circulated around the room to make sure everyone was on the correct page, concentrating on the students who might get confused with the format.

Just minutes before time was up, however, the teacher walked by the desk of Ronnie, the top math student in the class, and gasped. She saw him working diligently and saw that he would not finish. He had not understood the directions. Ronnie scored thirty percentile points below his ability level, and only because of an unfamiliar format.

Figure 9.1 is a simple version of what the math page looked like. The sign indicates the type of problem:

1. +	6. -	11. ÷
2. +	7. -	12. ÷
3. +	8. -	
4. +	9. X	
5. -	10. X	

Figure 9.1.

Ronnie, instead of working top to bottom as the numbers indicated, worked as he had been taught in class, from left to right. He finished items the top two rows across and two items in the third row. He took so much time working on the division problems that he had no time left for many of the easier addition and subtraction problems.

The reason many students do not do well on tests is that they, like Ronnie, do not understand the exact directions. The students must be sure that they understand the directions. Students become confused when test format or test directions differ from what they have encountered daily in the classroom.

Test-taking skills need to be incorporated into students' learning activities from the first day of school. However, parents must be informed as to the procedures used in grading papers. In one school, the teachers, as part of the test preparation program, all agreed to mark students' daily work as correct only if the student followed the directions exactly. This was explained to the students, and teachers did sample worksheets together with their students.

Parents may choose to follow this procedure with work done at home after checking with the child's teacher as to policies used at school. A second-grade teacher in that school told the students to underline the correct answer on a worksheet. One student circled each answer and received a 0 on the worksheet. The student's mother came storming into the principal's office the next day demanding that the grade be changed to 100 because the answers were all correct. The reason for the 0 grade was explained to her. The teacher had previously sent home a newsletter to parents explaining the purpose of this lesson. "But the answers are correct!" she repeated. She was then asked whether she preferred that her child receive a 0 on one worksheet now or a low score on a standardized test later because the child did not follow the directions exactly. She understood and reluctantly agreed.

The following are tips that students should be taught to follow when taking tests:

1. Scan the whole test or section before beginning in order to:

   • Become familiar with the test
   • Check the difficulty of the questions (are they the same throughout, or do they progress from easy to hard?)
   • Get an idea for pacing (how long is the test, and how much time is allowed?)

2. Always pay attention to the sample questions in order to:

   • Know exactly how to do the section
   • Identify any key words in the directions
   • Clarify oral directions

3. Ask before you begin if you don't understand the directions completely!

   • Remember: The test directions are written very specifically and have to be read exactly as they are written in the test manual. The

test giver is told what to say and how many times the direction may
be repeated.

ACTIVITIES

These activities can be used to teach students about the importance of following directions. Some of these activities may seem irrelevant; however, young
children first learn a skill through concrete activities. Then they progress to
paper and pencil tasks.

Classroom Lessons

What Is It? (Primary Grades)

Give students a worksheet containing the game chart found in appendix C
and the following directions.

1. Color B-2 blue.
2. Color F-2 and F-6 yellow.
3. Color B-3, B-4, and B-5 red.
4. Color D-2 and D-6 red.
5. Color B-6 blue.
6. Color E-2 and E-6 green.
7. Color F-3 and F-5 purple.
8. Color C-2 and C-6 orange.
9. Color F-4 brown.

What is it? _____

Find the Buried Treasure (Intermediate Grades)

Give students a worksheet containing the game chart found in appendix C
and the following directions.

1. In B-2, draw a tree.
2. From that box, go across five boxes and put an X there.
3. Go down seven boxes and draw three pieces of gold.
4. Follow the trail of gold pieces to find the buried treasure:

   - Go two boxes to the left and draw a large gold piece.
   - Go up two boxes and draw another gold piece.
   - Go two boxes to the left and draw five little gold pieces.

5. Go to the right one box and then up three boxes. Draw a picture of the shovel that the pirates left.
6. Go three boxes to the left and draw the treasure chest, for this is where the treasure is buried.
7. What box are you in? _____
8. Are you right? _____

Surprise (Primary Grades)

Give the students a worksheet titled *Surprise* that contains the following directions. Instruct them to read the worksheet and follow the directions.

1. Read everything before doing anything.
2. Write your name at the top of the paper.
3. Draw a square at the top of the paper.
4. Circle number 7.
5. Draw a line under your name.
6. Say your name out loud.
7. How old are you? _____
8. Stand up and sit down again.
9. What color do you like best? _____
10. Count to ten out loud.
11. Do only numbers 1 and 2

Surprise (Intermediate Grades)

As with the primary grades, give students a worksheet titled *Surprise* that contains the following instructions. Tell them to read the worksheet and follow the directions.

1. Read everything before doing anything.
2. Write your name in the upper right hand corner of the paper.
3. Write the date under your name.
4. Draw two small squares in the upper right hand corner of the page.
5. Write the name of your school on the bottom of the page.
6. Draw a box around the name of your school.
7. Raise your left hand and make a circle in the air.
8. Print your first name backwards. _____
9. Stand up and sit down again.
10. Shake hands with the person sitting next to you.
11. Count from one to ten out loud.
12. Write the name of your best friend. _____
13. Now that you have finished reading everything, do only numbers one and two and turn your paper over on your desk.

Hands-on Activities

1. Play Simon Says.
2. Give the students step-by-step directions to create an object using origami, the art of paper folding. (Books containing examples of this art may be found in the school library or possibly on the Internet.)
3. Play an activity record, CD, or video for the students, and have them physically follow the oral directions. (This is a great bad weather day activity that helps get the wiggles out.)
4. Give students step-by-step directions for an art or craft project. Holidays are prime times to use this activity.
5. Play The Gingerbread Man. To do this, read the story *The Gingerbread Man* to the class. Tell the students that the class is going to look for the gingerbread man, for you saw him that morning. You have already arranged what happens next. Take the class to where you supposedly last saw the gingerbread man. The person or a written note at that spot will tell the class that the gingerbread man left there and went to another location. Continue for a few more stops. One teacher used the principal's office as the last stop. When the students arrived, they asked in unison, "Have you seen the gingerbread man?" The principal responded, "Yes, he's been waiting for you!" That morning the teacher brought in enough gingerbread cookies for each child to have one. The cookies were then distributed to smiling, surprised children.
6. Follow a recipe. For example: make Jell-O following the directions exactly, and make another box using only cold water.
7. Read a play and make a list of the directions the actors must follow for the play to be a success. (Most basal reading textbooks contain at least one play written for that grade level.)
8. Have the students follow exact directions for writing a secret message. Put some lemon or orange juice in a small jar or bowl. Using a toothpick or the handle of a paintbrush, write a message on a blank sheet of paper by dipping the writing tool in the juice. Let the paper dry for a few hours. Hold the message up to the light or place it against a window and the message will appear. For the secret message to show, the directions must be followed exactly. (Note: If it is too close to the light, it may burn.)
9. Send students in teams on a treasure hunt around the school. Give each team the first direction. They will get the next direction at the first stop, and so on. Time, grade level, and facilities dictate the number of stops. Remember to notify the principal that students will be out of the classroom, and obtain prior permission of the other adults involved in the activity.

Written Activities

1. Give the students a copy of part of a road map. Start with a map of their town and progress to a map of your state and then to a map of the United States. Following your oral directions, students will trace or highlight the path from one site to another. For older students, the directions may be in written form. This type of activity will appear as a question in the social studies portion of a test.
2. Follow-up activity: After using the maps of the state and United States, instruct the students to plot a trip from Point A (the teacher's choice) to Point B (again the teacher's choice). Discuss routes the student might choose. Then using the "maps" section on the Internet, print out the route specified there. Discuss any differences.
3. Use the test direction vocabulary words (see chapter 2) in written assignments.
4. Give specific directions for a worksheet or workbook page. Your directions may differ from those written on the page. For example, you might tell students to write only the answer, circle the answer, or mark the two best choices.
5. Use a worksheet containing a picture with figures outlined in black. Then give specific directions for coloring it. Give oral directions for young children and written directions for older students.
6. The students will create a code for writing a message, for example, A = 1, B = 2, and so forth. Then they write messages using the codes they created, trade papers and codes, and decipher the message.
7. Each child gives the directions for his or her favorite recipe. The step-by-step directions may be written by the child or dictated to a parent volunteer or teacher aide. Remember to stress the proper sequence of steps for the recipe. Have the child then illustrate each recipe, and put all the recipes into a book that will be a Mother's Day gift. It will be a treasured cookbook in mom's collection.
8. Give the students a prompt for a writing assignment. Use a prompt that asks how or why, or that asks the student to tell a story in proper sequence. Examples of such prompts include, "You arrive home and find an unmarked delivery truck in your driveway. What do you think is in it?" and "Tell about your favorite field trip." Discuss whether or not the student answered what the prompt asked.

POINTS TO REMEMBER

- Match the test question with the number on the answer sheet.
- Read the directions slowly, carefully, and TWICE.

- Follow the directions exactly as stated.
- Sometimes part of the test is to determine whether directions are followed as written.
- Make sure you know the rules for marking the answer—that is, do you bubble in, underline, circle, make a check mark, or mark it with an X?

Chapter Ten

Guessing: Narrow to Two or Eliminate Incorrect Choices

Sammy sauntered into the house, opened the refrigerator, and very matter-of-factly said to his mom, "We started those tests today. But I didn't know some of the answers and I didn't want to read the rest, so I just marked anything."

How many of us have done that? As adults, we have had to learn how to select an answer on a test when we had absolutely no clue as to the correct answer. We acquired this skill through trial and error. Today's students do not have the luxury of time to learn as we did. The skill of guessing intelligently must be used as early as first grade.

This chapter deals with teaching students two skills: 1) to narrow the choice to two and then guess, and 2) to eliminate all the answers they know are definitely wrong and then guess from what is left.

The first step is to consider the following attributes of the answer choices.

- If two of the possible answers sound alike, look alike, rhyme, are opposite, have similar meanings, or begin with the same sound, then one of them is probably the answer.
- For true/false and yes/no questions, if all the information in the statement is true, then the answer is true. If any part of the information is false, then the answer is false.
- When matching columns of information, the student should match everything he or she knows and then guess from what is left.
- When eliminating wrong choices, the student should eliminate every choice that is not stated in the same terms as the question. For example, if the question asks for how many days, the student should eliminate responses given in terms of months, weeks, or hours.

The following examples show the process of eliminating incorrect answer choices.

1. Which fruit is red?

    ○ Ketchup
    ○ Apple
    ○ Hot dogs
    ○ Banana

    The student should eliminate all items that are not red ones and then choose the fruit, or eliminate all items that are not fruit and then select the red one.

2. Mark the answer:

    2
    3
    +4
    ——

    ○ 5 [add 2 + 3]
    ○ 234 [all three numbers written together instead of added]
    ○ 9 [correct]
    ○ 7 [add 3 + 4]

    Discuss with students why each of the three wrong choices is inappropriate and should be eliminated.

3. Which shape has four equal sides?

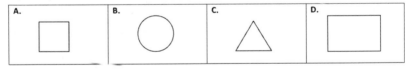

    ○ A
    ○ B
    ○ C
    ○ D

    The student should use the key words *four sides* to select choices A and D, and then use the key word *equal* to select A as the correct choice.

ACTIVITIES

Activity 1

The smaller the number of choices, the better the chance of getting the correct answer. Play the following game: Write a number from 1-50 on a piece of paper, and put the paper face down on the desk. As each student guesses what the number might be, write their guesses on the board. After everyone has guessed, show your paper and tally how many students guessed correctly. Do the same activity with 1-25 and 1-10. The smaller the number choices, the greater the chance students have of getting the correct answer.

Activity 2

This activity set is for very concrete learners, but will help others as well.

Exercise A

Select four students to stand at the front of the room: two wearing no blue clothing, one wearing a blue shirt, and one wearing blue jeans. Ask, "Which child is wearing a blue shirt?" First, ask students to identify the key words in the question (blue, shirt). Second, ask them to eliminate students not wearing blue. Third, two choices are left; ask the question again. Call on a student to give the correct answer and then ask why the person wearing the blue jeans is not the correct choice. Repeat the activity using other attributes of people or pictures, such as size, shape, height, hair or eye color, things that fly, or things that grow.

Exercise B

Teach the skill of narrowing down the answer choices in a lesson using attribute blocks. Each block in a set has four attributes: color (red, yellow, or blue); size (big, little); shape (circle, square, rectangle, or triangle); and thickness (thin or thick). They can be purchased at a toy, discount, or department store. Put four blocks on the table and ask a student to select a block with a particular attribute. Then ask for another block, this time specifying two attributes. Depending on the cognitive level of the students, increase the selection to three and then four attributes. For example, you might give students these directions:

1. Point to the large blocks.
2. Point to the thin squares.
3. Point to the small red square.
4. Point to the large thin red square.

Exercise C

A fun, challenging game (more so with intermediate students) is to build a train of the blocks on the floor of the classroom. Begin by putting the engine (first block) of the train down, and then select a student to add the next car. Say, "Look at the engine. Now select a block that has one attribute [or two, three, or four attributes] different than the engine." For example, if the engine is a large, thick, red square, the student might pick a small, thick, red square. The next student might then pick a small, thick, red circle. When the selection of blocks remaining to choose from lessens in number, the game becomes far more challenging. Allow students to help each other.

Activity 3

Give the students a teacher-made worksheet with several statements important to the reading, science, or social studies chapter that they are currently studying. Have students use the skills they have learned for deciding whether an answer is true or false to write *true* or *false* after each statement. Students should then write the page number in the textbook where the fact is documented.

Activity 4

For homework, assign students a passage to read in any one of their textbooks. They should then write two statements about the passage, one true and one false. Again, students should document the statements with page numbers. The students' statements may be used as test questions for that chapter of the text. Use the question, but do not identify the name of the student who wrote it.

POINTS TO REMEMBER

- Identify the key words in the question.
- Narrow the choices to two and then guess.
- Eliminate the answers that you know are wrong and guess from the choices that are left.
- Work backwards. Match the answers to the questions.
- If you have no idea as to the correct answer, choose one letter (e.g., "B" or "C") and mark that chosen letter each time. You have a better chance of getting some correct than if you select a different letter each time. (This strategy is helpful for students taking the SAT or ACT.)

- Some tests have a penalty for a wrong answer (e.g., ¼ point for each wrong answer). Ask before you start the test. This rule is found in tests at the high school level and above (SAT or ACT).
- Math: Read the sign before each problem. Some tests put like examples in a selection while others mix up the type of problem. Answer choices often include answers for problems, but with a different process (e.g., subtraction answer for an addition problem).

Chapter Eleven

Guessing: Judging Answers

"Guess what?" Beth excitedly asked her mom as she burst through the front door. "My friend taught me a new word today, 'Christmas treeing.'"

Noting the puzzled look on her mom's face, Beth continued explaining her revelation. "I don't mean like the one we decorate at Christmastime. We took those long reading tests today, and Sue told me that if you don't feel like reading all that stuff, you could just mark any answer. It's called Christmas treeing. I guess that's because the paper looks like the lights on the tree, with marks all over the page." She then proudly stated, "I was the first one done!"

A very upset mom and dad told this story in the principal's office the following morning. Fortunately, the test was not a major assessment but simply a publisher's periodic reading test given after the first section of the reading book was taught. Beth and Sue were allowed to retake the test in the guidance counselor's office, during the time they usually had recess. The entire faculty used this opportunity (without mentioning names or the incident) to discuss with their students why it is so important to read a test and then use the test-taking skills they have learned in order to select the best answer.

When using guessing skills (see chapter 10), some students still may be confused or even overwhelmed by the choices and may have difficulty making a selection. In order to narrow the choice to two or eliminate wrong answers and then guess from the remaining choices, the students need to learn how to evaluate or judge the responses.

- Is the answer written in the same terms as the question (e.g., feet/yards, dollars/cents, days/weeks)?
- Does the response answer what the question asks (e.g., who = person, when = time, where = place)?

- Is the response mentioned in the story (e.g., the story discussed a bike ride and the answer talked about a car)?
- Does the response satisfy the key words in the question (e.g., "What could not really happen?" the answer must be something that is not realistic or possible and could *not* really happen)?

ACTIVITIES

1. Play the game Hold Everything. This is particularly effective when used as a review for a test. Select the pages in the reading, social studies, or science textbook to be considered. Allow the students to ask questions of the teacher or parent about the material. This can be done with open books. The answers will vary, sometimes being factual and sometimes being fictional or incorrect. When a fictional or incorrect answer is given, students must say aloud "Hold everything!" Students love this game, and they can get quite boisterous. Next, reverse the process and ask the students questions. The students will try to outdo each other with the most outrageous answer. However, once the answer is recognized as fictional, the student has to give the correct answer and then verify it by citing the exact page and paragraphs in the text.

2. Present a picture from a textbook, magazine, or poster. Discuss what the picture tells the viewer. Lead the students to answers that are factual as well as fictional or incorrect. Again, ask the students to document their responses. For example, show a picture of a little boy sitting on the grass holding a bruised knee, with a tricycle tipped over next to him. An incorrect answer would be that the boy looks happy. The documentation would be the tears on his face or the bruised knee.

3. Use old tests to teach the skill of evaluating answers. Let the students discuss the merits of each value choice. This is also the time to point out that they should read every answer choice to make sure their selection is the best one.

4. Play the game *Jeopardy!* as seen on television. The teacher may create his or her version of the game using textbook material, or an electronic version may be purchased to practice the skill of judging answers.

Chapter Twelve

Working Backwards

A substantial portion of the choices on a first-grade assessment test used in an elementary school were in the form of pictures. Students had a tendency to select a picture that had at least one object in it that was mentioned in the question. A new test preparation program was implemented before the "assessment test week" in one county school system. At the end of the week, the first-grade teachers in one of the schools marched into the principal's office with big smiles rather than their usual demeanor for the end of test week, which was sheer exhaustion and some frustration. All four of the first-grade teachers had observed that their students would point to each picture, either shake or nod their head, move on, and finally select the best answer. They had used their newly taught test-taking skills of judging answers, working backwards, and guessing. This scenario was repeated in several of the other schools in the district.

There are times when a test taker does not know a word or words in the question. The student then has a tendency to just mark any answer. The following activities can be used to teach students to use the information in the answer choices to guide them in making their response. This skill is called working backwards.

ACTIVITIES

Activity 1

Begin with a concrete example. Select four children to come to the front of the room, two girls with blonde hair, one girl with black hair, and one boy with black hair. Ask, "Which girl has ebony hair?" The responses will vary and include shrugs, puzzled looks, blank looks, and the question, "What does ebony mean?" Lead the students to use the four answer choices to make their selection:

- First, because the question said "girl," eliminate the boy.
- Second, the answer must be one girl only, so eliminate the two girls with blonde hair.
- Third, select the girl with black hair. The students do not have to know what *ebony* means in order to make a good choice.

Repeat the activity with other attributes of people and objects.

Activity 2

This activity is best explained by displaying the questions and answer choices on the chalkboard or on paper. Display a question such as the following:

What word is the opposite of b _ d?

- o Run
- o Big
- o Pretty
- o Good

Discuss each answer choice separately. Because students do not know the word in the question, they should let the beginning and ending sounds of the word be a guide as they evaluate the possible answer choices. As students suggest words that mean the opposite of *run*, write the suggestions on the board. Check the list to see whether there is a word starting with *b* and ending with *d*. Repeat the procedure with each selection. Then, continue with the following:

What is the opposite of s _ _ p?

- o Yes
- o Open
- o Go
- o Hello

Because students do not know the word given in the question, they must look at each of the answer choices and give its opposite (yes/no; open/close; hello/good-bye; go/stop). They can then evaluate the opposites to see which one matches the beginning and ending sounds of the mystery word.

What is the opposite of n _ _ _ t?

- o Up
- o Day
- o On

o Hot

Again, students should look at the answer choices and give the opposite of each one (up/down; on/off; day/night; hot/cold), then choose the word whose opposite matches the beginning and ending sounds of the mystery word.

Point out that sometimes the choice will come down to one of two and guessing will be the only way in which to select the answer. Use choices written at the student's independent reading level so that the students will then concentrate on the test-taking skill, not the academic material.

Activity 3

Play the game *Jeopardy!* as seen on television. This is especially effective when reviewing reading, science, or social studies material. The students will need their textbooks for this activity. The teacher states the fact (an answer) and students must state the corresponding question or must find the exact words on the page that tell what the question should be. The student who correctly says the question will state the next answer, and so on.

Activity 4

Find an old worksheet or test and use correction fluid to hide some words or letters in each question. Then copy the worksheet or test for students to complete using the newly learned skill of working backwards.

POINTS TO REMEMBER

- Read the question first.
- Select the key words in the question.
- Read all four answer choices.
- Eliminate the answers that do not match the key words.

Chapter Thirteen

Key Words

Five classrooms of fifth graders were surveyed concerning their feelings about taking tests. One of the survey questions was, "I could do better on tests if ____." One girl responded quite honestly, ". . . if I didn't pay so much attention to the boys."

Reliable tests do not have trick questions, as some test takers believe, but they do have important words or phrases that are called key words. It is advantageous for the test taker to become aware of these words and learn how they make reading the questions and selecting the answer understandable.

Elementary school children know what a key is and what it does: it unlocks something. In tests, key words are used to unlock the information in the question to make selecting the answer easier and quicker. Just as your front-door key will unlock only your front door, a key word will unlock only the correct answer.

There are three steps in the process of using key words to help select an answer to a test question:

1. Identify the key word or phrases.
2. Match the key word or phrase to each answer choice.
3. Select the correct answer (using the skills discussed in chapters 10, 11, and 12).

Make a list of the key words and save it in your favorite type of format. Either print or technology will suffice, but use a format that is easily access-ible for reference often. Encourage students to devise a system for maintain-ing and adding to their own list of key words. This can be done with a small notebook, small note cards, or typed and saved on a hand-held technical device. Add to the list as more key words and phrases are identified throughout the school year. Words to begin with are *not, always, never, seldom, mostly, more, less, when, where, why, who, what, how, best answer, in all, all together, have left,* and any other basic words important to the subject matter of the curriculum.

Another area in which it is vital that the student know the meaning of the key words is in both the instructions for the specific section of a test and in the test questions. Children may have difficulty understanding that instructions and directions can be stated in many different terms. The skill is particularly challenging for early elementary students—that is, first and second graders. There is a wide variety of words used to tell the student how to designate an answer choice. They need to be taught that *mark, select, bubble in, fill in, blacken, color in, shade,* or *darken* are the terms used in directions and that these words all mean the same thing. They may know how to *draw a line under* but become thoroughly confused when told to select a word that means the same as *the underlined word.*

In standardized tests, the test directions to the teacher often do not permit either a repeat of the direction or a clarification of it, and they have to be stated to the student exactly as written in the testing manual. When giving the students teacher-made or textbook tests, use the same rules so the students become familiar with the process. Also, incorporate the same terminology throughout the school year. This is not "teaching the test"; it is "teaching test-taking skills."

Use the following commonly used test question vocabulary and subject matter terms as a starting point for helping the students become familiar with the terminology and, thus, become more familiar and comfortable with the test:

General:

- Circle, space, oval, shape, figure
- Column
- Not, not true, false
- Sample
- Best
- Box
- Probably
- Only
- Diagram, graph, chart, table
- Corresponding space
- Key words
- Always, almost always, most likely, mostly, sometimes, often, never
- Correctly, correct way
- Symbol

- Items
- Timed test

Reading:

- Passage, story, paragraph, selection, sentence, phrase, statement
- In this story, refers to, in this passage
- Summary, summarize, main idea, all about, mainly about, tells about, describes
- Compare, contrast, similar, the same, different
- Verb, noun, adverb, adjective, punctuation, tense
- Synonym, opposite, antonym, goes with
- Sounds like, rhymes with, the same sound
- Underlined word, underlined letters
- Sequence, order in which things happen, best order
- Cause, effect
- Opinion, fact, true, false
- Choice, none, none of these, none of the above, not here
- In real life, cannot really happen
- Makes sense
- Bold face, italics, dark print
- Stands for, the same as, another way of saying, almost the same as, closest in meaning

Math:

- Problem, item, word problem
- Equal to, equivalent, another name for, rounded to
- Number sentence, fraction
- Symbols ($+$, $-$, $\times$, $<$, $>$, $=$, etc.)
- Beginning, middle, end, next, finally, last, before, after
- First, second, third, etc.
- Top, bottom, front, back, over, under, between, next to, behind, in front of, above, below
- Place value
- Area, mass, volume
- Circle, square, rectangle, oval, triangle
- *Addition*:
    - About how many, how many, all together, in all, how many have then, how much
    - Total, sum
- *Subtraction:*

- o How many (much) more, how many (much) less
- o Difference, how many are left
- o Most, more, less, least

- *Multiplication*:

  - o Times, each, how many in all

- *Division:*

  - o What fraction, what part
  - o Divided into, divided equally
  - o Each, how many in one
  - o Average

Science:

- Tables, graphs, charts, diagrams
- Describes, characteristics of, function
- Observations, results, purpose, main purpose, method
- Cell, organism, mixture, solution, object

Social Studies:

- Describes, function of, main purpose
- Cause, effect, result of, reason for
- Time line

The meanings of some of these words may seem obvious, but that might not be so for elementary students. Remember, do not assume. When in doubt, double check whether the student has a good grasp of the meaning of the word or phrase in the context in which it is used in the test.

ACTIVITIES

Hands-on Activities

1. Teach students how a key unlocks information, as in a map, a chart, or a mystery novel. On the board or paper, write students' suggestions of what a key opens (door, padlock, jewelry box, car trunk, diary, luggage). Make a second list of information that can be unlocked. Examples include maps, charts, mystery novel, phonics, context clues, word attack skills, math signs, spelling rules, science procedures, codes, and language rules.

2. Have students make their own list of key words to keep for reference when learning testing strategies or when doing class work. Options for the list include the following:

   - Small spiral notebook (student purchased) that easily fits into the desk or backpack
   - Computer-printed list
   - Index cards: one word or phrase to a card, with cards kept together in a plastic bag, inserted into a recipe box, or held together with a rubber band
   - Booklet made from paper and stapled together

3. Play the game Simon Says. Identify key words used in the game.
4. Select a mystery story to use in reading class or to read aloud to students. Students will identify keys that will help solve the mystery.
5. Using a road map of the town, students use the key to determine the distance from their home to school or to each other's homes. This information may be found easily on the Internet or on hand-held devices. However, students need to have a background of the process involved in order to fully understand the process.
6. Have students make an attribute-block train as described in chapter 10, activity 2, exercise C. Have students listen for key attributes when selecting the next car in the train.
7. Have students do an art or craft project. Give directions one step at a time. Students identify the keyword or phrase in each step that tells them what to do to finish the project, for example, *cut*, *paste*, *draw*, and *fold*.
8. Students will read a play and select the key words that tell the actors what to do, where to move, and what facial expressions and tone of voice to use when speaking. Have students act out the play while ignoring these directions. Then have students act out the play following the directions exactly.

Written Activities

1. Have students underline the key words that give directions on their daily homework worksheets.
2. During social studies and science lessons, read the questions at the end of each chapter. Have the students identify the key words before answering the questions.
3. Have students read advertisements from magazines or the local newspaper. Ask them to highlight the key words in the ads that will entice the reader to purchase the product.

4. Have the students read a recipe and highlight the key words in the recipe.

POINTS TO REMEMBER

- "Always, never, and not" mean with no exception.
- "Most, sometimes, mostly, seldom, rarely, may, may be possible" mean some exceptions are possible.
- Math: In word problems, look for the key words that indicate the type of computation needed.
- Any word that is in **bold print**, *italicized*, or underlined is important.
- There are three steps in using key words for success:

    1. Identify the key words or phrases.
    2. Match the key words or phrases to each answer choice.
    3. Select your answer.

Chapter Fourteen

Selecting Multiple-Choice Answers

Once the students have mastered the individual strategies discussed in chapters 10, 11, 12, and 13, the next step is to combine these skills in a logical, sequential order. Elementary school teachers are adept at identifying students who have difficulty transferring material from one genre to another. These are the students who pick out the key words in a math test question but haven't realized that the same skill is equally effective in reading, social studies, or science tests.

The following technique is for all students, but particularly for those who want the test-taking skills put into practical, logical, user-friendly terms. This technique, which needs to be used often and in every area of the curriculum, is called FOCUS. The first step is to verify that the students at your grade level recognize and comprehend all the words in the acronym. Then proceed with the step-by-step strategy.

FOCUS

F—Find Key Words

The student should begin by identifying key words in the question. The most commonly used key words are listed in chapters 2 and 13. Beyond that, each textbook series has words that are indigenous to that particular subject. Add these key words to the basic list. Possible sources to consider are:

- End of chapter questions in social studies and science
- Periodic or cumulative tests that accompany the reading textbook
- Word problems in the math textbook
- Teacher-made classroom tests

O—Omit Wrong Answers

First, the student should omit the choices that do not confirm the key words in the question (see chapter 10). Next, omit answers that misstate the facts in the passage (see chapter 11).

C—Change Direction: Work Backwards

Next, the student should identify any answer choices that contain words or phrases beyond his or her recognition or comprehension level. Then, the student should use the context clues in the rest of the answer to determine whether or not this choice may be a possible correct response (see chapters 11 and 12).

U—Use Guessing Clues

If only one answer is the logical response, the student should go to the next step "S," and select and mark the choice. If there is more than one possible answer, the student should make an intelligent guess (see chapter 10).

S—Select and Mark the Answer

Correctly and completely mark the answer.

ACTIVITIES

1. Expose the FOCUS technique to the students by including the words from the acronym in classroom spelling and vocabulary tests.
2. When the students are off task, stop and say FOCUS!, and then continue with the lesson in progress. The procedure will both remind the students what they should be doing at the time and reinforce the word.
3. Require students to list or underline the key words in each question in classwork or homework assignments.

SAMPLE TEST ITEMS

Use the following three sample test items as a guide in teaching students to use a step-by-step procedure when taking multiple-choice tests. Lead them to the realization that the same procedure is applicable regardless of the subject matter. For your classroom, select passages from the textbooks in all areas of the grade-level curriculum. Collaborate with your teammates in writing the test items. The school district's testing coordinator may be able to supply you with old tests that may be used for practice.

Sample Reading Test Item

Peanuts grow best in sandy areas where it is warm. President Jimmy Carter grew up on a peanut farm in Georgia. When he was a young boy, his father taught him how to raise peanuts. He sold the peanuts to earn spending money.

Peanuts are sold in many places as snacks. They may be found in candy, ice cream, and snack bars. Peanut butter sandwiches are a favorite for lunch. But there are some people who can't eat peanuts because they get very sick.

There are over 300 uses for peanuts. Peanut oil is used in cooking. Peanuts are also used in making soap, ink, and paint. Peanut butter can even be used to remove gum from your clothes.

What is the main idea of this story?

A. Everybody likes peanuts.
B. President Carter resided on a farm.
C. Peanuts have many uses.
D. Peanuts can grow anywhere.

Use the steps of FOCUS to select the correct answer.

F—Find Key Words: The key words in the question are *main idea.*
O—Omit Wrong Answers: A is a wrong answer. The story stated that everyone can't eat peanuts because they get sick. D is a wrong answer. The story stated that peanuts grow best in warm sandy places.
C—Change Direction: Work backwards: In choice B, the student may not understand the word *resided.* Using the context clues in the sentence and working back to the story, the student is able to substitute *lived* for *resided.* B is true according to the story, but it is not what the story is all about, so it is a wrong answer.
U—Use Guessing Clues: A, B, and D have been eliminated as correct answers. Therefore, C is the answer.
S—Select and Mark the Answer: Correctly and completely mark C on the answer sheet.

Sample Social Studies Test Item

In the future, many people will travel in space. Astronauts had to learn how to do many things in a different way. They will teach space travelers what to do.

There is no food or water in space. It has to be brought from Earth. Some water has to be recycled so it may be used again. Otherwise, the supply may run out. The food is brought in packages or cans. Water is added to some of it before it is heated in a microwave oven. There are foods such as macaroni and cheese, soup, and even cookies. But there are no peanut butter and jelly sandwiches. The breadcrumbs would float around and get into the equipment.

Space travelers sleep in bunk beds or sleeping bags. But they have to be attached to the bed or the wall. They don't want to fly around and bump into things.

Some things will be the same. For fun, space travelers may bring CDs and CD players to listen to music. They bring DVDs to watch movies. They even play checkers.

What is the most important way space travel is different from earth travel?

A. Space travel will be more fun.
B. There will be no peanut butter and jelly sandwiches.
C. There are no souvenir stores.
D. Everything you need must be brought with you.

Use the FOCUS procedure to arrive at the best answer.

F—Find Key Words: The key words in the question are *most important* and *different*.

O—Omit Wrong Answers: A is a wrong answer. Space travel may be more fun for some and not for others. This is not most important.

C—Change Direction: Work backwards: Students may not know the word *souvenir* in choice C. The words *no* and *store* are familiar. Buying souvenirs may be fun, but it is not most important. This is a wrong answer.

U—Use Guessing Clues: B and D are left. B is in the story, but it is not most important. This is a wrong answer. As for choice D, if you forget something (e.g., food), you can't go to the store to buy it. This is very important.

S—Select and Mark the Answer: Correctly and completely mark D on the answer sheet.

Sample Math Test Item

Mom baked sixty cookies for the party. The children ate twenty-seven of them. How many were left?

A. 87
B. 33
C. 47
D. Not applicable

Use the steps in FOCUS to find the correct answer.

F—Find Key Words: The key words are *were left*. That means the problem is one of subtraction.

O—Omit Wrong Answers: A is the answer if both numbers are added. The problem is subtraction. C is the answer found if the subtraction is done incorrectly.

$$\begin{array}{r} 60 \\ -27 \\ \hline \end{array}$$
$$7 - 0 = 7$$
$$6 - 2 = 4$$

This answer would be 47. Therefore, both A and C are wrong answers.

C—Change Direction: Work backwards: In choice D, the student may not know the word *applicable*. However, this might be a possible answer if the other three choices are all wrong.

U—Use Guessing Clues: D is a possibility. But the computation for B needs to be completed: $60 - 37 = 23$. This is the correct answer to the subtraction problem.

S—Select and Mark the Answer: Correctly and completely mark B on the answer sheet.

POINTS TO REMEMBER

F—Find key words.
O—Omit wrong answers.
C—Change direction: work backwards.
U—Use guessing clues.
S—Select and mark the answer.

Chapter Fifteen

Pacing

A first year teacher of second graders worked diligently teaching her students test-taking skills. Before the yearly standardized assessment test, she read the manual twice, rearranged the furniture in her classroom, took down charts that might be advantageous to her students, reviewed what materials the students would need, and finally retaught her students how to bubble in answers. At the end of the first day of testing, she went to the testing coordinator in tears. Her students were being so meticulous in the process of bubbling in the correct answer that they did not finish the test in the time allotted.

The next morning, before she passed out the tests, she discussed this with her students. She used the current terminology and told them that she had stressed it too much. She said, "Be cool! Bubble in and move on!" The students heeded her advice.

Standardized tests have a component not often found in classroom work: time limits. There is no opportunity for the student to finish the work later in the day or to take it home for homework. Students not taught pacing skills tend to either work at a carelessly fast pace or ignore the time restraints and turn in unfinished papers.

Pacing is a difficult concept for right-brained students. They tend to flit from one task to another. These tasks are all brought to completion, but in their own time frame. With these students, first stress the need for the skill. Then, begin teaching it in short time frames. Increase the time frames as the students' comfort level allows.

The following activities will help the students develop an accurate concept of time, thus alleviating test anxiety and resulting in test scores that correctly indicate their skill level.

ACTIVITIES

Concrete Activities

1. Use the math timed test that is found at the end of this chapter. Discuss the activity with the class.
2. Cover the classroom clocks for the day. Students who wear watches will need to remove them for this lesson. Throughout the day, stop and allow students to guess what time it is. Repeat this activity periodically.
3. Give the students five minutes to talk, play a game, or work on a fun project. Do this activity on a day when the clocks are covered. Tell them that they have five minutes, and after the time is up, discuss their concept of the time period.
4. Do the same thing as in activity 3, but assign a tedious written worksheet. Again discuss their concept of time.
5. Using a chart, have the students create a list of activities that would require pacing. Some examples are a race, a sporting event, a swimming competition, the student lunch period, the time needed to get to an appointment or to school, meal preparation, and a television program. Discuss the importance of pacing in each situation. Post the list on the classroom wall and add to it as students discover more activities that need to be done in a specific time frame.
6. Have students calculate the number of problems that will need to be completed in the allotted time in order to finish a math worksheet. For example, to finish fifteen problems in half an hour, two minutes are allotted per problem.
7. Before each activity performed in the classroom, allow students to estimate the time required for the task. Discuss criteria for making this judgment: 1) the number of problems or questions that are included in the task or worksheet; 2) whether the task requires filling in the blanks, writing a word or phrase, or writing complete sentences; 3) in math, whether the student must show all work or write only the answer; 4) whether the material is an easy or hard subject area for the student; 5) whether the student feels prepared; 6) how tired the student is (is it morning or afternoon?); and 7) whether there are distractions in the room.

Written Activities

1. Time homework assignments. Send home a flyer to parents with directions as to how to do this activity with homework and with household

chore assignments. Begin by allowing much more time than needed. Gradually, lessen the time to a realistic limit for the assignment. In the case of household chores, parents should set the time so that students will have to stay on task and work diligently in order to finish.

2. Assign class work in which the difficulty level varies throughout the assignment. Time the lesson so the students will have to skip the hard problems in order to finish. Lead them to the conclusion as to why this strategy is advantageous in getting a higher score. Devise a system with them to indicate the number of problems they skipped so they know how many to come back to if time allows. Also, stress that they must check periodically to make sure the number of the problems matches the number on the answer sheet.

TIMED MATH TEST

There are two forms for this computation test. Form A begins with problems that are difficult and progresses to easy ones, and Form B contains the exact same problems, but with the easier ones first. You can make your own similar test using problems from the student textbook.

Give half the class Form A and the other half Form B. Give them three minutes to complete the page. Adjust the time allowed according to the level of difficulty of the problems. Do not tell the students that there are two forms. Tell them that this is a lesson on how long it takes to finish.

After time is up, ask how many completed all sixteen problems.

Allow students to compare the two forms and let them discover why the scores differed. Then lead a discussion as to how students can alleviate this situation and ensure that they complete all the problems they are able to do. Suggest the following techniques:

- Scan the test before beginning to see if the problems go from easy to hard, left to right, top to bottom, or in random order.
- Skip the hard questions, returning to them later if time allows.
- Use skills learned in guessing for the difficult questions.
- Use skills learned in working backwards to select the answer choice.
- Double check that the answer choice being bubbled in has the same number as the question.

Math Timed Test: Form A

1.) 5 / 25	2.) 8 / 56	3.) 6 / 45	4.) 12 / 144
5.) 3 × 2	6.) 7 × 7	7.) 13 × 4	8.) 21 × 15
9.) 9 − 4	10.) 7 − 2	11.) 18 − 6	12.) 46 − 31
13.) 3 + 4	14.) 8 + 7	15.) 14 + 3	16.) 37 + 19

Math Timed Test: Form B

1.) 3 + 4	2.) 8 + 7	3.) 14 + 3	4.) 37 + 19
5.) 9 − 4	6.) 7 − 2	7.) 18 − 6	8.) 46 − 31
9.) 3 × 2	10.) 7 × 7	11.) 13 × 4	12.) 21 × 15
13.) 5 / 25	14.) 8 / 56	15.) 6 / 45	16.) 12 / 144

POINTS TO REMEMBER

- Ask whether or not the task is timed—and for how long.
- Don't "amble" (work too slowly) or "scramble" (work too fast).
- In lengthy tests, if you have absolutely no idea as to an answer choice—skip that question. Use your predetermined answer choice (see chapter 10) and move on.
- When answering questions about a passage, read the questions first. Then read the passage. Then read and answer the questions. This does save the time you spend searching for the answer. (*Note:* Elementary students are taught to "read and find out." Thus, read the questions first to "find out" what to look for when reading the passage.)
- If the section is timed, skim for format, content, and length. Then proceed accordingly.
- If you have time left, go back and fill in those you skipped, making sure you match the number of the question to the number on the answer sheet.

- Ignore those who finish early and are proud to be the first one finished. You are not competing against them—you are working for yourself.
- CONCENTRATE ON YOU AND YOUR TEST—NOT ON THE OTHERS IN THE ROOM.

Chapter Sixteen

Math

An assistant superintendent of a school system arrived unannounced to observe a fifth-grade teacher who was in contention for the district's Teacher of the Year award. She was just beginning a test-taking skill lesson on following directions. As she passed out the worksheets, she also handed one to the visitor.

She simply said, "Begin now and do what the directions tell you to do."

This was the paper used:

1. Read everything before doing anything.
2. Write your name in the upper right-hand corner of the paper.
3. Write the date under your name.
4. Draw two small squares in the upper right-hand corner of the page.
5. Write the name of your school on the bottom of the page.
6. Draw a box around the name of your school.
7. Raise your left hand and make a circle in the air.
8. Print your first name backward _____
9. Stand up and sit down again.
10. Shake hands with the person sitting next to you.
11. Count from 1 to 10 out loud.
12. Write the name of your best friend.
13. Now that you have finished reading everything, do only numbers 1 and 2, and turn your paper over on your desk.

After a few minutes, some giggling was heard, and students began looking around the room to see what everyone else was doing. As the assistant superintendent read number seven on the paper, he stopped, scanned the rest of the page, and burst into a hearty laugh. Like all the students, except two, he had started working without following the written directions.

For days afterward, the students delighted in talking about the educator who didn't follow directions any better than they did. The lesson stayed with them, and they became adept at following written and oral directions. The assistant superintendent used the incident as a teaching tool when working with his principals.

The math sections of required criterion based tests present challenges that students do not usually encounter in the classroom. The material tested follows the curriculum taught in the classroom and found in the textbooks adopted for use in the school system. Once the students have learned the material, they can concentrate on the test format used in presenting the material.

The areas tested in the math portion of the test include numbers and operations (computation), measurement and data analysis, geometry, and algebra. Some states add other domains as they deem necessary. A large portion of this section is using problem-solving skills in reading and interpreting diagrams, charts, tables, and graphs.

The first of the three principal challenges is that of using key words related to math terminology (e.g., *how much more*, *how much less*, and *how many in all*, as well as *graph*, *chart*, *table*, and *diagram*). Reading and heeding these words, as listed in appendix F, will lead the students to the correct function or strategy to solve the problem at hand. Both identifying these words and knowing of the meaning represented by them are needed in the process of arriving at the correct answer.

The second challenge is the ability to budget one's time and pace oneself throughout the timed sections. In a classroom setting, students finish as many problems as time allows, but then they may complete the work later in class or take it home for homework. This is not so in a timed math standardized test. Knowing the test is timed causes anxiety even in the best of students. By teaching pacing strategies while using the student's required math curriculum, both pacing and math skills will be strengthened.

The third challenge is that of dealing with several functions in the same subtest—that is, addition, subtraction, multiplication, and division problems on the same page. The anecdote at the beginning of this chapter illustrates the importance of following the exact directions. In this case, math signs must be followed exactly. On a classroom worksheet or textbook page, the same computational skill will generally be used throughout the lesson. Tests, on the other hand, often vary the type of math computation problem within a section. Reading signs is especially important because of the nature of the answer choices on a multiple-choice test.

For example:

17
− 8

- o 11 [subtract 8 − 7, then 1 − 0]
- o 136 [multiply 8 × 17]
- o 25 [add 8 + 17]
- o 9 [correct answer]

This skill may be reinforced throughout the daily work by requiring students to compute math problems with varying functions. The important strategy is teaching the awareness of the math function.

Stress the following general tips:

- Check for the key words.
- Watch the signs carefully.
- Ask yourself if the answer should be smaller or larger than the original numbers.
- On scrap paper, rewrite problems in familiar format. For example, when given the problem $10 − 5 =$ _____, rewrite it as

10
− 5

- Follow the number sequence carefully. Are the numbers arranged vertically, in columns, or horizontally, in rows?

ACTIVITIES

Estimating Activities

1. Students often need additional school supplies. Use the prices of the items in the school store or from the local newspaper ads to estimate what it will cost to purchase these items. Do the same with other items that a child might purchase, such as clothing, CDs, and software.
2. Most schools have book fairs periodically to support the purchase of new books for the school library. Each student is given a brochure of the items for sale (books, posters, and magazines). After returning to the classroom from their walk-through of viewing the materials, teach the students how to both estimate and calculate the cost of their selections. These lists are taken home to parents who edit the selections and

provide money for the purchases. Before the students go to the library for purchasing, assist them in computing the actual costs of the materials and the amount of change to be received from the money the parent has allowed. Another lesson learned here is the computing of the state sales tax.

3. Many teachers use commercial book clubs for students to order books and software economically. Follow the same guidelines used in activity 2 for this activity.
4. Use everyday situations to create oral word problems. For example:

   - Our family has 2 children. If each child brings a lunch 3 days this week, how many lunches will we need to pack?
   - 3 students live in our home. Mom wants to order 2 number-two pencils for each student for the standardized tests. How many pencils will need to be ordered?

5. Using information from your book fair or book club flyers, create word problems. For example:

   - How much more does [title of book] cost than [title of another book]?
   - I have $20.00. I bought [title of a book] and [title of another book]. How much change will I get back?
   - How much less is the least expensive book than the most expensive book?

Pacing Activities

1. Use the activities in chapter 15.
2. Conduct math relay races. Divide the classroom into teams. One person from each team goes to the board. The teacher then states a math problem. The first person to write the correct answer earns a point. The functions used in the problem should be varied so that students practice the skill of being aware of the math sign.
3. Put time limits on some homework and class work. When beginning this skill, allow more than enough time for all students to finish. Gradually lessen the time allotted.

Sign-Reading Activities

1. While traveling to school or around the school campus, make a list of all the posted signs. In the classroom, discuss the purpose of each and what would happen if people did not do what the sign says.

2. Make a worksheet of the format on a math test. Guide students to see that the answer choices are correct for other functions. That is, the problem may be subtraction, but the answers are given using choices for addition, multiplication, and possibly a combination of the original numbers.

    Examples:

    $$\begin{array}{r} 18 \\ -\ 7 \\ \hline \end{array}$$
    ○ 25 ○ 11 ○ 18 ○ 2

    $$\begin{array}{r} 12 \\ +\ 4 \\ \hline \end{array}$$
    ○ 12 ○ 7 ○ 16 ○ 8

    $$\begin{array}{r} 8 \\ \times\ 3 \\ \hline \end{array}$$
    ○ 24 ○ 11 ○ 5 ○ 38

    5/35
    ○ 175 ○ 1 ○ 40 ○ 7

3. Create a worksheet of math problems, including the answers. But do not put in the sign. The student's task is to put in the proper sign. For example:

    $$\begin{array}{r} 15 \\ \underline{?7} \\ 8 \end{array}$$
    ○ + ○ − ○ × ○ ÷

    10 ? 2 = 5
    ○ + ○ − ○ × ○ ÷

Key Words Activities

1. Make a list of key math words (see appendix F). Use a chart, small spiral notebook, or note cards. This may be one list or several; each geared to a particular function. Students should keep the list handy when doing homework or class work.
2. Create oral word problems using familiar facts. Before computing the problem, students must identify the key words. Examples:

- Our Little League team has _____ players. Three are absent today. How many are playing today?
- Our team has _____ players, and the team we are playing has _____ players. How many players are there altogether?

3. On written work, require students to circle or underline the key words. Remember to follow exact directions.

POINTS TO REMEMBER

- Become familiar with all charts, tables, diagrams, and graphs found in the math textbook. The tests are filled with these images for the test taker to interpret and then answer questions concerning the data.
- Learn the terminology for all the images as well as the terminology for computation and problem solving.
- Identify the key words in the questions.
- Pay attention to the math signs.
- If the test is timed, pace yourself accordingly.

Chapter Seventeen

Social Studies and Science

Jan gave her dad her latest social studies test on US history. Dad looked at the "D" grade and then looked back at his daughter. "Well?" he asked.

"I did all my homework and studied hard," Jan responded defensively. "But when I took the test, my search button didn't work."

Social studies and science are each an important component of the state criterion referenced tests. With the stress on science and math skills, some states consider the science score part of their criteria for promotion. Check with your child's classroom teacher as to the whether either of these subjects is considered in the promotion decisions.

Each state has developed its own syllabus (an outline of the course of study) for each grade level from kindergarten through twelfth grade. The state then either creates its own test or purchases one that will meet their needs from a testing publishing company. The test must measure the student's mastery of the material contained in the school system textbook. Many states begin the testing of science and social studies as early as second grade and then periodically at specified grade levels. Appendix B lists each state's web address for access to the information you need for your child.

For each subject, ask the teacher for access to a copy of the grade-level textbook. The teacher's role is to teach the student the contents of the textbook over the course of the school year. The parent's role is to supplement what the student learns in class. Particular emphasis should be placed on reinforcing and reviewing the terminology and vocabulary specific to the subject. The glossary of the textbook is very helpful in this area. The other area of reinforcement is that of understanding and interpreting charts, tables, graphs, and diagrams. These graphics are used throughout all the areas tested. Chapter 18 of this book gives examples and explanation of what the student will be exposed to on the tests.

As you search your state's website, look for the answers to these questions concerning the science and social studies tests:

- In which grades are these tests given?
- What specific areas of information are covered? (Many state websites will list the specific skills covered.)
- Are the tests given in one or more settings?
- What types of graphics are used in the test questions? (These may be found on the practice tests.)
- How many questions are on the tests?
- What types of questions are used (multiple choice, completing graphics, fill in the blanks, etc.)?
- Explain the scoring system and what constitutes pass/fail.
- Is either of these tests criteria for promotion? If so, which ones, and what is the test score needed for that promotion?

Locate the practice tests on the state website and print them out. Allow the child to take the test in paper/pencil format similar to what the child will experience on the test. When the student has finished, use the answer information found following the practice test. Go over it together. This lesson is invaluable. Not only are the correct answers given, but reasons are given for why that answer is correct, as well as why the other choices are incorrect. For additional review and to add to the test-taking experiences, go to the websites of other states and print out their practice tests and follow the same procedures.

Science and social studies make use of diagrams and tables to compare and contrast information in a specific genre. Seeing the information in a graphic is helpful to all types of learners. Venn diagrams (see chapter 18) are typically used in science class to show similarities and differences of elements, wildlife, or forms of vegetation. This type of graphic is used in the tests in all areas: science, social studies, and reading.

Some tests still ask questions about using reference material; that is, the dictionary, encyclopedia, and atlas. Expose the child to these sources. This may require a trip to the local library. The more information a test taker has when taking a test, the less of an anxiety level will be experienced and the more confident the student will be.

USING A TABLE OF CONTENTS

Teach this skill when using any textbook the child is using at school. Typical questions asked on tests are the following:

1. Which chapter tells about _____?
2. On what page would you begin reading to find out _____?
3. How many pages are in the chapter called _____?
4. To learn _____, on which page will you begin reading?
5. What is the title of the chapter that begins on page ___?
6. Chapter ___ would probably tell about _____?

USING AN INDEX

Use the textbook index often to teach mastery of this skill. Typical questions asked on tests include the following:

1. On what page would you find information about _____?
2. Where will you look to find information about (name of a person)?
3. What pages tell _____?
4. What page gives you the definition for _____?
5. Which word is an antonym of _____?

POINTS TO REMEMBER

- Websites for each state are in appendix B.
- Key vocabulary and other terminology are in chapter 13.
- Graphic examples and explanations are in chapter 18.
- Review the glossary of the child's textbook in each subject area.
- Expose the child to print maps (the United States, his or her home state), as that is the format the child will encounter on a paper/pencil test.
- Ask the reference librarian in the children's section for books that contain subject matter corresponding to that in the science or social studies textbook (e.g., American history, stories of children living in other climates or lands, stories dealing with science subjects).
- Involve technology as much as possible when teaching research skills.
- When selecting websites, let key words in the description of the site be your guide.

Chapter Eighteen

Maps, Graphs, Tables, Charts, and Diagrams

A sixth-grade teacher informed her students that, in two weeks, they would have an end-of-chapter social studies test. The students knew what those tests were like, so they diligently completed their homework, read and reread pages in the text, and quizzed each other on details. They knew it would be hard.

When the day arrived, the teacher announced that the test would be given right after lunch. When the students walked back into the classroom from the cafeteria, they noticed that the big US map was pulled down to cover the test questions that were written on the chalkboard. The teacher told everyone to get out two sheets of paper and a pencil. She even waited while a few students sharpened their pencils.

When everyone was ready, she pulled up the map. On the board, in big letters, was written "April Fool's!" One student summed it up best when he shouted, "Wow! That's the best April Fool's joke I ever had!"

That situation actually happened several years ago. In talking to the student who shouted out his appreciation for the joke, he still visualizes the room, still remembers where he sat, and still can see the teacher release the map to show those words. Many testing situations, like this experience, are very memorable. Teachers today, having to meet the high standards of society (as did teachers years ago), now have to give many standardized tests to document their accountability and students' mastery of the learned material at that grade level.

Each section of a standardized test contributes to the score reflected on the total battery (a group of several tests). Previous tests had just a few questions that included maps, graphs, tables, charts, or diagrams. With the importance of technology in the twenty-first century, the ability to read these visual aids is vital. Graphics in today's tests have become the norm rather than an infrequent addition to the math or social studies portion of the test. Examples of these graphics can be found at every grade level and in every area of the curriculum.

A *graph* is a diagram that can help us compare things. The form of the graph depends on the type of information being represented. There are four types of graphs: line graphs, bar graphs, circle graphs, and pictograph.

A *map* is a picture of an area; that is, it is a drawing that represents the Earth's surface. Maps come in many forms. Primary students begin with picture maps and intermediate students study road maps, physical maps, political maps, and relief maps.

A *table* is made of words and numbers and takes up a small space. If the same information were put into words alone, it would take many paragraphs. Tables compare information and are easy to read.

A *chart* depicts several items, and questions relating to the chart require the reader to use the properties of the pictures to tabulate information. Charts are particularly effective with primary students with limited reading skills. They are primarily used in math.

A *Venn diagram* is a sketch, drawing, or plan that explains something by depicting parts and their relationship through graphics.

The comprehensive tests use these graphics at all grade levels and in all subject areas. The test taker "reads" the graphic and answers questions about the information depicted on it. The best way to learn to "read" these graphics is to learn to create them.

Sources for creating graphics:

- Type in the name of the graphic in your search engine. Look for sources that are specifically geared to elementary students.
- In Microsoft Word, click: Insert > tables. Use their formats or create your own.
- In Microsoft Word, click: Charts. The list contains all types of graph formats to create.

The rest of the chapter will give samples, examples, and concrete activities for each type of visual aid. The students' textbooks or the Internet are the best sources to view or create any of these visual aids.

ACTIVITIES

Bar Graphs

Bar graphs show how different quantities compare to a given source or to each other.

1. As a homework assignment, have the student check the kinds of shoes everyone in the house is wearing. Graph each pair according to slip-ons, sneakers, sandals, boots, and shoes with laces. In the classroom, graph the types of shoes each child is wearing.
2. Use bags of M&M's for this project. Because the students will eat the candy at the end of the lesson, the number of candy pieces distributed to each student depends on the number of students. The students will graph the number of each color of candy. The results can then be put into a table to see whether the bag has an equal number of each color or to see which colors predominate.
3. For a social studies lesson, assign each student to research the population of three cities in your state. Once the populations are determined, teach the students how to put the coordinates on a graph.
4. After a vacation or field trip, list the favorite attractions of each family member. Put each choice in the form of a bar graph so students can see everyone's favorites.

Line Graphs

Line graphs show trends or changes over a period of time or over an area.

1. Graph the student population of each grade level in the school or in each classroom on a particular grade level. The students will research the statistics.
2. Check with the cafeteria manager each day for the number of lunches sold. Graph these numbers for a month. This will indicate to the students what the favorite meals are for the school.
3. Graph the temperature each day for a month, making sure it is taken at the same time of day. Another activity would be to take the temperature every hour the students are in class, for one day only. This graph can have two lines: one for the projected temperature and another for the actual temperature.
4. Graph the snowfall or rainfall for several days. Again there could be two lines, as in activity 3.

Pictographs

Pictographs use actual pictures to represent the data.

1. Have each student draw a picture of his or her favorite toy on a sticky note. Then have the student place the sticky notes on the graph (a poster or the chalkboard) according to color. Other pictures, such as

animals, favorite foods, fruits, or birds, can be used and can be categorized according to color, size, or category.
2. In March, make a calendar and put either a lion or a lamb on each day. At the end of the month, graph the days of each type. Graphing can also be done with cloudy, sunny, rainy, and snowy days.

Circle (Pie) Graphs

Circle or pie graphs show relationships of parts to a whole, usually in percentages.

1. Calculate the expenses for a vacation or field trip: transportation, gas, entrance fees, meals, hotels, and souvenirs. Add each amount to get the total, and then calculate the percent each amount is of the total. Intermediate students can put these percentages into a pie graph on the computer.
2. Check with the cafeteria to get the number of students buying lunch and the number buying only milk. Use total enrollment figures to calculate the number bringing lunch from home. Compute the percentages and put them in a pie graph.

Tables

Tables are charts that contain data about sets of different items.

1. Make a table titled "Report Card Grades." The columns contain the report card grades (A, B, C, D, F, or E, S, N, U, or 95, 90, 85, 80). The rows list the subject areas. Only total numbers of students are used, no names. Ask the type of questions about this table that students would encounter on a test. For example:

   - How many students received Cs?
   - What grade did the most students receive?
   - How many more students received Bs than As?

2. Use other information from school for other tables:

   - Lunches sold, for example, hot dogs, spaghetti, hamburgers
   - Number of students who go to bed at each of four times (teach tallying)
   - Political election data (number of voters per grade level, per precinct, or per state)
   - Number of books sold in the book fair (five or six favorite titles and the number sold of each)

- School population (number of grade levels and number of class-rooms per grade level)

Maps

Maps show roads, population density, and land use.

1. Take a walk around the school neighborhood, taking note of where landmarks are located. Then have students make a map of the neighborhood.
2. Tour the neighborhood and, again, make note of the landmarks. Have students make a three-dimensional map at home, using cardboard cartons, popsicle sticks, blocks, clay, and fabrics.
3. Plan a vacation or field trip. Use the actual road map and highlight the route. When actually traveling, give each student a copy of the necessary part of the map so they can follow the charted path.

Charts

Charts show properties of objects.

1. Using a menu from a local restaurant, ask questions that require students to compute and compare prices.
2. Select five items from the classroom (or use items sold in the school store). Make large price tags for each. As in activity 1, create several addition and subtraction problems using these prices.
3. Display four items: a ball, a book, a triangular block, and a square box. Ask questions that require students to identify properties of the items, for example, shape, number of corners, or number of sides.

Venn Diagram

A Venn diagram shows relationships between sets.
    Use the format for either two or three circles.

1. Reading: Select any two characters in a story in the textbook or library book. Another option would be to use a character from one story versus a character from a different story. This activity greatly increases comprehension.
2. Science: Check the textbook and select categories from that grade level. Some examples include birds versus bats, shrubs versus trees, winter versus summer, electricity versus gas, or house pets versus wild animals.

3. Social studies: Examples include country versus city living and mountainous versus beachfront living.
4. Transportation: Examples include things with and without wheels and things that go in the air versus things that go in the water.

EXAMPLES

The following visual aids are examples of the type of items found on standardized tests. Use the maps found in social studies textbooks for practice with maps.

Circle Graph

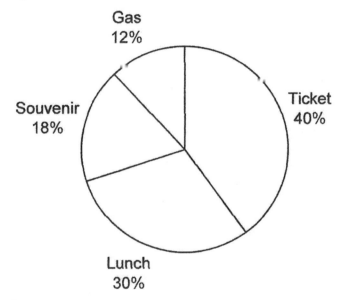

Figure 18.1.

This graph is in the shape of a circle or pie and shows the relationship of the parts to the whole. It is particularly useful when working with budgets. The key indicates what each pattern represents. Each pattern in the graph shows the percent of the total cost for each item.

Each student paid $30.00 to go on the field trip. This graph shows how the expenses were divided. Sample questions:

1. What costs the most?

    ○ Ticket
    ○ Souvenirs
    ○ Lunch

      ○ Gas

2. What item costs less than the souvenirs?

      ○ Lunch
      ○ Gas
      ○ Ticket
      ○ Souvenirs

3. What two items equal over 60% of the total cost?

      ○ Lunch and gas
      ○ Gas and souvenir
      ○ Lunch and souvenir
      ○ Lunch and ticket

Line Graph

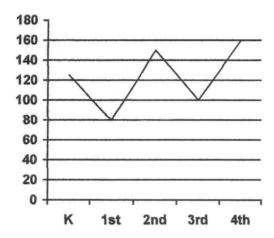

Figure 18.2.

A line graph uses a line to show a pattern of facts. The value of this type of graph is to show upward and downward trends at a glance.

At an elementary school, the number of students at each grade level varies. This type of graph predicts the number of teachers, classrooms, and textbooks needed for the following school year. Sample questions:

1. In what grade level are the most students?

      ○ 2nd
      ○ 3rd
      ○ K
      ○ 4th

2. How many students began in kindergarten?

  o 175
  o 100
  o 50
  o 125

3. In what grade level are there the fewest students?

  o K
  o 4th
  o 1st
  o 2nd

Bar Graph

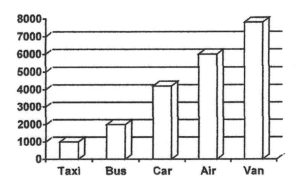

Figure 18.3.

This graph uses bars to show how different quantities compare. The value of bar graphs is that the comparison can be seen at a glance.

Many people traveled to the championship soccer game. The graph shows how many came by taxi, bus, car, airplane, and van. Sample questions:

1. Most people traveled by:

  o Airplane
  o Van
  o Taxi
  o Car

2. About four thousand people traveled by:

  o Taxi
  o Bus
  o Van
  o Car

3. More people traveled by bus than by:

o Air
o Car
o Taxi
o Van

Pictograph

Rectangle

Triangle

Circle

Square

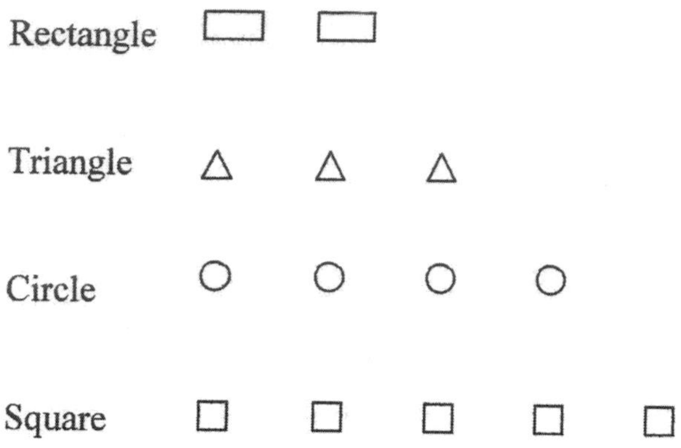

Figure 18.4.

A pictograph uses pictures to show information. Sample questions:

1. Which type of shape was drawn the most?

   o Rectangle
   o Triangle
   o Circle
   o Square

2. How many students drew circles?

   o 1
   o 4
   o 2
   o 5

3. Which shape was drawn less often than the triangle?

   o Triangle
   o Circle
   o Rectangle
   o Square

Table

Number of Pages Read for Homework

Students	Reading	History	Science	English
Ann	10	15	10	4
Bob	5	14	10	4
Cal	25	10	0	4
Donna	12	20	8	2
Ed	15	16	6	2

A table is a chart that contains information about sets of different things. The title of a table shows what the information represents. Sample questions:

1. Which student read the most pages in reading?

    ○ Ann
    ○ Bob
    ○ Ed
    ○ Cal

2. Who read the least number of pages?

    ○ Bob
    ○ Cal
    ○ Donna
    ○ Ed

3. How many total pages did Ann and Donna read in history?

    ○ 25
    ○ 10
    ○ 22
    ○ 35

Venn Diagram

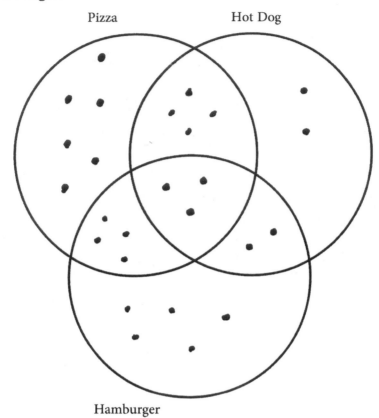

Figure 18.5.

1. How many students like only pizza?

    ○ 2
    ○ 3
    ○ 4
    ○ 6

2. How many students like all three foods?

    ○ 2
    ○ 3
    ○ 5
    ○ 6

3. How many students like just hot dogs and hamburgers?

    ○ 2

○ 3
○ 4
○ 5

POINTS TO REMEMBER

- Check the practice tests from several states to see a variety of graphics.
- Create your own graphics.
- Check textbooks for graphics and make up test questions for them.

Chapter Nineteen

Comprehension

As a third-grade teacher circulated around the classroom during the reading comprehension portion of the yearly standardized assessment test, she noticed that Ken was sitting with his hands folded and a big grin on his face. She walked over to his desk, leaned over, and quietly whispered, "What's the matter? Why aren't you working?"

His grin turned into a smile, and he responded, "That was too much reading, so I guessed just like you taught me." Then he proudly added, "I'm the first one finished!"

Ken's favorite subjects were lunch, recess, and physical education. Putting time and effort into a reading test were not a priority for him at that time. But, the real underlying reason for his performance was that he was not a proficient reader and the format of the reading test overwhelmed him.

Sound familiar? Reading and social studies teachers, particularly, worry about students who have shown in their daily work that they have the capabilities for completing these sections of the test but who look at the test format and are overpowered with a sense of defeat.

There are four sequential strategies to practice when working on reading comprehension on any test, whether literature or social studies. In order for these strategies to be used effectively and with confidence, the students need practice, practice, and more practice. This can be done using the student's textbooks. The four strategies are as follows:

1. First, read the question. A student retains more information when provided with a purpose for reading.
2. Read the passage twice. These passages will have unfamiliar material, but they are not lengthy, and the allotted time is usually generous.
3. Read the questions and identify the key words. (Refer to chapter 13.)

4. Use guessing strategies. (See chapters 10, 11, and 12.)

In a classroom, after students have read a selection from a textbook, the teacher questions them to check comprehension of the passage. The questions are either factual or critical-thinking questions that expect the student to recall information. Standardized tests, because they are scored electronically, are formatted so that the student selects the correct answer choice from four possibilities. These are two different skills. In the classroom method, the student sends out information to the teacher in answer to the question.

The testing method, in contrast, has three steps: first, the student takes in four pieces of information; second, the student considers (processes) the choices; and third, the student sends out the answer to the question. Being able to answer a question using one of these methods does not always transfer to being able to answer the question using the other method. Elementary school students need to be taught from the concrete to the abstract, thus, they need to be taught both ways. The first method of answering a direct question is a natural process for young students. The testing method is foreign to elementary students, and it needs to be taught in a step-by-step process. Walk the student through the process of selecting the correct answer from a choice of four possibilities. Remember to discuss each choice as to why it is either correct or incorrect. Be consistent and repeat the process often.

ACTIVITIES

The best way to teach comprehension is to follow the weekly format described in chapter 5. The contents generally contained in the reading comprehension portion of the test are main idea, making inferences (a particularly difficult skill), cause and effect, sequence, locating information, getting facts (the easiest concept), drawing conclusions, and the author's purpose for the story. The skills in this section of a standardized or criterion referenced test, being the most challenging for the students, must be a priority in the following:

1. Main idea

    • What is the main idea of _____?
    • What is the best title?
    • What best tells about the story?
    • What is the story mostly about?
    • What is the topic of the story?

2. Author

- Why did the author write this selection?
- What was the author's point of view?
- What was the author's opinion of _____?
- How did the author feel about _____?
- What did the author mean by _____?

3. Fantasy versus reality

- What can happen in real life?
- What cannot really happen?
- What could not be true?

4. Sequence

- What happened first in the story?
- What happened next/finally/last in the story?
- What happened just before _____?
- What happened just after _____?
- Put these sentences in order as they happened in the story.

5. Cause/effect

- (Effect) happened because (cause).
- The main character (effect) because (cause).

6. Inferences/drawing conclusions

- What did the character/author mean when he or she said _____?
- Why did _____?
- The main character felt (emotion) because _____?
- The mood of the passage was _____?

7. Getting facts

- Where?
- When?
- Who?
- What fact tells _____?

The importance of this activity can't be stressed enough. Select the reading passage, choose a concept, and write five test questions, one for each day of the week. Remember to select a passage at the student's independent reading level, that is, material the student both reads and understands easily (see the following example). In each of the seven areas listed previously, assign one type of test question for the week. Compile these to create worksheets used in practicing reading comprehension test-taking skills. Material from a recently read library book may also be used for this activity.

Reading Levels

Reading Level	Percent of Comprehension	Percent of Word Recognition
Frustrational	50% or less	90% or less
Instructional	50%	90%
Independent	90–100%	90–100%

POINTS TO REMEMBER

- When teaching any test-taking skill, use material from a previous grade level. After the student has learned the test-taking skill, select material at his or her grade level.
- Teach the student to identify why one answer is correct, and why each of the other choices is wrong. Learning this skill is invaluable.
- Follow these four steps for each reading passage:

    1. Read the questions first.
    2. Read the passage twice.
    3. Read the questions again and identify the key words.
    4. Use the guessing strategies previously learned.

Chapter Twenty

Sequencing

Teachers of first- and second-grade students who had limited writing skills often allow them to give their book reports orally. It was common for a student to say: "First . . . and then . . . and then . . . and then . . . The End." The report was one very long run-on sentence, but the sequence of the story was usually quite accurate.

Students of that age are able to retell the story in sequential order. They also are able to read four sentences about the story (not listed in proper sequence) and number them from one to four in the correct order. However, because of the methods of scoring, standardized tests present the questions on sequencing in a more complex format. This is a step beyond the format used in the classroom.

The following test directions are typical of the format for a question on sequencing:

Which of these is the *best* way to organize the following sentences in the correct order?

1. The next day they went to the beach again.
2. Then they saw an old bottle in the sand and took it home.
3. First, they picked up some pretty shells.
4. They threw the bottle in the water and hoped someone would find it.
5. Sue and Dan went to the beach.
6. They wrote a note and put it into the bottle.

> A. 1 2 3 4 5 6
> B. 2 4 6 1 2 3
> C. 4 5 2 3 1 6
> D. 5 3 2 6 1 4

After reading the directions for a test item of this type, the teacher looked at the students and saw facial expressions that cried out, "Help!" This teacher was more frustrated than the students were, for the directions could be read only once and exactly as they were stated in the testing manual. The teacher knew no help was forthcoming to the students.

The students in that class had learned the skill of sequencing. They could both tell and retell a story from beginning to end in a logical sequence. They could recognize when a story was told to them out of sequence. They were proud of their mastery of the skill of numbering four sentences in sequential order. But this testing format threw them into a state of complete confusion. A question such as this tests their test-taking skills, not their knowledge of the correct sequence of the events in the passage.

The next school year, the teachers on this grade level worked together to write test questions in this format. They used the material in every area of the primary-grade curriculum. They put examples on the chalkboard, on paper, and in PowerPoint presentations. By test-taking time, the students were familiar with the format and thus only had to deal with the content of the material.

Sequencing is also tested by questions that ask when a particular incident happened in the passage. Understanding the terminology in the question will help students decide the correct answer. The following format is used for this type of question. Remember that students will be selecting an answer from a choice of four possibilities.

- What happened before _____?
- What happened after _____?
- What happened next?
- Where does the story start?
- Where does the story end?
- What happened first in the story?
- What happened last in the story?
- Which comes first?
- Which comes last?
- What happened just before _____?
- What happened just after _____?
- What did <u>(name)</u> do before?
- What did <u>(name)</u> do after?

There are many key words that will help students select the correct sequence for their answer. Make a chart with three columns: beginning, middle, and end. Using the words listed in the following, ask the students which words tell what could happen at the beginning, middle, or end of a story, and place them in the corresponding column of the chart. Keep in mind that some words may be listed in two sections; they simply tell what could not happen at the beginning or what could not happen at the end of the story.

After
After that
At last
Before
Begin by
Beginning
End(s)
Finally
First
In conclusion
Last
Later
Middle
Next
Second
So
Start
Third

Pronouns (he, she, they, we, it) are used only after the noun they represent has already been stated. Thus pronouns do not happen first.

ACTIVITIES

1. A quick and easy activity is to recap the day's activities. As the students recall each incident, write it on the chalk or marker board. The remainder of the activity can be done in two ways:

   - Use only four events. Number them one through four. Discuss.
   - Use four different events and ask the student to write them sequentially on paper. Discuss.

2. When students are to leave the classroom for home, lunch, or an activity, line them up a few minutes early. Then ask who is

   - First in line
   - Last in line
   - Standing next to (name)
   - Standing before/after (name)
   - Standing in front of /behind (name)
   - Second, third, fourth, fifth, and so forth

- At the beginning/end of the line

3. For a homework assignment, ask students to write four events that happened in the day's literature, social studies, or science lesson. Then they will number the events sequentially. These lists of events can be used for the daily activity in sequencing. Write them into your weekly lesson plan.
4. This activity is for students in the primary grades. Tell three students they are to come to the front of the room and line up as follows: (name) is last, (name) is in the middle, and (name) is first. Also use first/second/third, beginning/middle/end, or any other sequential order. Do not give the directions in the proper sequence. The students may seem confused as they get to the front of the room. The students in their seats will be very helpful in telling each child where to stand in line. It is a fun activity.

POINTS TO REMEMBER

- Teach sequence and test it in the same format as used in the standardized tests.
- Use grade-level textbook material when writing test items.
- Share the process with teammates. This lightens the workload and benefits all the students on that grade level.
- Use sequencing vocabulary (from the previous list) in giving oral directions.

Chapter Twenty-One

Writing

A fourth-grade boy came home from school one Friday clutching his writing folder. He had a great big smile on his face. His mom immediately became suspicious, for her son did not like school.

"Did you know there is a different system for grading stories?" he asked.

"Oh?" she replied with a great deal of skepticism.

"Yes!" he said excitedly. "A means awful, B means bad, C means careful, D means dandy, and F means fantastic." She gave him credit for being creative, and was relieved that his work was much better than she had expected.

Writing has taken on a whole new role in the elementary curriculum. Teachers are now taught in depth to teach writing skills to elementary students, beginning as early as kindergarten. This change was needed after a period inundated with workbooks, dittos, and black line masters in which the student simply filled in the blanks. Students were not required to write complete sentences or paragraphs.

Then the pendulum swung in a different direction, as it periodically does in the field of education. Computers don't have blanks to fill in: users are required to create and compose their thoughts when using the keyboard or in writing emails. Spelling, sentence structure, and the use of paragraphs became a required skill. Spelling was the easiest, as most writing programs contained spell-check. Help is available for correct sentence structure. When the green line suddenly appears under part of the writing indicating incorrect English grammar, the student has immediate access to the rules. An explanation of the rule (with examples) is given, thus the student has instant editing. Writing a variety of documents is part of the language arts curriculum in the schools.

But, then, the pendulum swung again with the popularity of texting and social media sites. Because of the restrictions of the number of characters in a message, texting requires an abbreviated form of word and sentence structure. The rules for correct English grammar and sentence structure became immaterial. However, the student will use these writing skills when availing themselves of the many other social media sites.

Writing has become a priority and a necessity. Students must not only do well throughout the school year, they must also demonstrate their mastery of writing skills, which is generally tested at the fourth grade in the elementary sequence. The scores on these tests are used to rate students, teachers, schools, and school systems. But the positive side is that teachers are being trained to teach writing skills, and as a result, students are becoming proficient writers.

States have put together task teams to write the criteria and prompts for their required, mandated tests. Teachers and other educators have been selected and put through a training regimen to score writing tests according to a specific set of guidelines. These tests, unable to be scored on a scanner, have subjected scoring that has been deemed accurate.

Most states require the writing tests of fourth graders. However, the teaching of the writing skills needs to be introduced in the beginning years of the elementary curriculum. There are four factors to be considered when teaching writing:

1. The genre of the written work
2. The elements of the work
3. The rubrics (scoring) of the work
4. Activities for students in preparing for the tests

Each state has its own specific guidelines. A copy of these guidelines should be made available to every teacher and parent. Some score on a scale of one to six and others grade on a scale of one to four. The rubrics are the same; the difference is the gradation of the skills for each score. The information in this chapter applies to all writing tests.

THE GENRE OF THE WRITTEN WORK

Children write for a variety of reasons. The genres for the tests seem to fall into three categories. Some states ask students to write on two different genres. In some cases, the students in a classroom are not all given the same writing assignment.

1. *Informative, expository, open-ended, or open response:* The student is expected to write to inform, clarify, define, explain, instruct, or report. A specific prompt is given to the students asking them to write in a variety of formats. The writing may be composed in the form of a report, a letter, a review, or an essay.
2. *Narrative, on-demand writing:* This genre is either factual or fictional and takes the form of a story. The student is asked to write about an experience or event.
3. *Persuasive writing:* The student in this case endeavors to influence the reader to take some sort of action. This action may be changes, improvements, permissions granted, or support for activities. Because the writer is persuading, the composition may contain reasons, documentation, examples, and comparisons.

THE ELEMENTS OF THE WORK

Holistic scoring is the process by which the writing compositions are graded. This means no one element has a greater weight than another element. The scorer looks at the work as a whole, not in separate parts. The thoroughness with which the four elements are incorporated into the work is the criteria on which the rubric score is based.

1. Focus: Focus refers to how the writer stays on topic without digressing. The subject has to be consistently and clearly maintained.
2. Organization: The organization is the plan of development, including a logical sequence of events. There has to be a very clear beginning, middle, and conclusion. Organization is evidenced by transitions from one thought to the next and the inclusions of supporting ideas.
3. Support: Support refers to all the details that enhance the topic. There are words that define, clarify, and explain. There is strong evidence of a varied vocabulary and mature word choice.
4. Conventions: Conventions are the following English skills:

   - Spelling
   - Punctuation
   - Capitalization
   - Legible handwriting
   - Complete sentence structure, including simple, compound, and complex sentences
   - Noun and verb agreement

THE RUBRIC OF THE WORK

A rubric is a scoring criteria at each point on a scale, just as a grade (e.g., A, B, C) or percentages (e.g., 80, 85, or 90 percent) is used in the classroom. The following is a guide to a four-point-scale rubric. A six-point-scale rubric evaluates the same skills but applies a finer division in the application of the elements.

Rubric 4

- Focus on the topic is complete and clear.
- Sequence flows logically from beginning to end.
- There is a sense of completeness.
- Vocabulary and sentence structure are effective and varied.
- The work shows an awareness of correct parts of speech and spelling.
- Correct punctuation and capitalization are used.

Rubric 3

All of the skills for Rubric 4 are displayed adequately with minor errors.

Rubric 2

- The writer adequately focuses on the prompt.
- There is evidence of digressing and extraneous material.
- There are some supporting details, but support is not complete.
- There is a loose attempt at sequence.
- Vocabulary and sentence structure are limited.
- Errors are evident in spelling, capitalization, and punctuation.

Rubric 1

The paper is poorly written with frequent and glaring errors in all areas. Focus on the topic is lacking.

ACTIVITIES

1. In class, assign a prompt and allow the same amount of time that will be allowed for the test.
2. Grade students' writing in the rubric format. Explain this system to students. The school system writing coordinator can provide guidelines for teachers as to how to score writing papers using this system.

Parents may ask for guidelines to use when critiquing their child's writing assignments.

3. Allow students to suggest prompts.
4. Make charts of descriptive words (adverbs and adjectives).
5. Have students practice varying the vocabulary used in their writing.
6. Provide models of all levels of writing. The school's or school system's writing coordinator should be able to provide samples.
7. Have students practice writing. Use the following sample ideas.

- Show the students a picture from the local newspaper or a magazine. Ask them to write a story to accompany the picture.
- Write a review of a school assembly, play, concert, or sporting event.
- Take a picture of a school activity and ask the students to write a story about it.
- Write a story about why homework is necessary.
- Write a letter to the principal requesting changes in a policy or procedure.
- Write a letter to the testing company stating opinions about tests.
- Write about a favorite day or event.
- Write a letter to their parent or guardian asking for permission to do something.
- Write about their favorite time of year.
- Describe their favorite room in the house through the five senses.
- Keep a daily journal.

DEFINITIONS RELATED TO WRITING TESTS

Conventions: The commonly accepted and appropriate rules of English, spelling, capitalization, and punctuation

Draft: The first version of a writing piece before revisions

Expository/open-ended/informative writing: Writing that explains, clarifies, defines, teaches, and generally gives information

Focus: The point of concentration on the topic

Holistic scoring: A method of evaluating the composition as to its overall quality

Narrative/on-demand writing: Factual or fictional writing that tells a story sequentially

Organization: Development of beginning/middle/end and the process used to progress from one thought to the next

Persuasive writing: Writing that attempts to motivate a reader to a specific action or viewpoint

Prompt: A writing assignment that directs the writer to a specific topic

Rubric: A set of criteria for each score point of the scale

Support: Evidence and facts pointing to the central topic of a piece of writing

POINTS TO REMEMBER

- Ask for the school system's printed guide (some may have it on their website) for the rules and procedures of the writing tests.
- Promote the use of new vocabulary words in speech and writing.
- Encourage students to write reviews on Amazon or Barnes & Noble book websites of books they have read.
- Encourage students to write letters to their elected officials about issues concerning them (insist on a positive, respectful format, although the content may deal with negative issues).
- Teach the student how to critique other writings (in the newspaper, in a magazine, or on the Internet) and assign the task as a homework assignment. Parents may work with the student in accomplishing this project.

Chapter Twenty-Two

Everyone's Role: Teacher, Parent, Student

Some of these guidelines are repeated in each list for they are a responsibility of each group. This is to ensure everyone gets the message of the importance of their role in supporting the student.

FOR THE TEACHER

To be accomplished during the school year:

1. Use practice worksheets in daily classwork and homework that are written in testing format.
2. Notify the office of the times there are to be no interruptions: no intercom, no parents, no late students. Tell students prior to the test that no one will be admitted to the classroom once the test has begun.
3. Give tests throughout the school year using the practice tests on the state's website (and from other states' websites).
4. Make no changes in the classroom the week before the test to eliminate new distractions: do not rearrange furniture, do not change bulletin boards, and do not wear a new clothing style or have a new hairdo.
5. Take notes the day of the test. Was the student ill, did the student's dog die, or was there an upsetting family incident that morning?
6. Explain to the students why they will be taking these particular tests.
7. Tell the students when the results will be available and who will get them.
8. Explain to students whether the test is written in such a way that some of the material might be too difficult for them.

9. Explain how the results will be used.
10. Explain how make-ups will be handled.
11. State whether the teacher can answer questions once the test has begun. Use these same rules in giving tests throughout the school year.
12. Remind students that a late student will not be allowed to enter the classroom once the test has begun.
13. A week before the test, ask the students, "Are you a tortoise or a hare?" Read them the story and discuss the traits of each and how those traits helped or hindered. Relate the traits to test taking.
14. Review the skills learned:

   - Guessing skills
   - Read questions twice
   - Read questions, then passage, then answers, and follow guessing skills
   - Follow directions exactly
   - Use time wisely

15. Send a flyer to parents stating:

   - The dates of the tests
   - The times of the tests (remind parents that latecomers will not be allowed into the testing room once it has begun)
   - What test is being given
   - Why the test is being given
   - When they may expect to receive the results

16. When tests are being given, all phones must be turned off. This is an absolute must.

   NOTE: Send a general flyer at the beginning of the school year stating each test's name and date. Before each specific test, send the flyer with data for that test, including the supplies needed by each student.

FOR THE PARENT

Ask the teacher to explain the following:

1. What tests are given
2. When the tests are given
3. Why the tests are given
4. When they can expect their child's results

5. Definitions of terms they need to know in order to understand the results

6. To send a well-prepared student to school on test-taking days, see to the following:

- Sleep: See that the child goes to bed at his or her regular time. Too much sleep is just as detrimental as too little sleep.
- Breakfast: See that the child eats his or her regular breakfast. However, children who do not eat breakfast should eat something on the day of the test.
- Clothing: See that the child wears comfortable clothing and also the clothing that is his or her favorite. Check the weather for the day.
- Materials: Provide the child with three number-two pencils and an eraser.
- Be on the child's side: Send the child to school knowing you want the child to do his or her best and you will support the results.

FOR THE STUDENT

1. Come to the test prepared:

- Bring three [AQ1]number-two pencils (two dull points and one sharp point) and an eraser.
- Take care of bathroom needs before the test.
- Have tissues handy.
- Wear comfortable clothing (check the weather).
- Get the amount of sleep you require to be able to do your best work.
- Eat breakfast to meet your needs. (Protein and carbohydrates are needed for energy. Avoid sugar and caffeine.)

2. Think about the techniques and strategies you learned to beat test-taking anxiety.

3. Review the following test-taking skills:

- Are you a tortoise or a hare? (To the teacher: Read the story to the class and discuss the traits of each and the advantages and disadvantages of working too slowly or too fast.)

4. Use your guessing skills.
5. Read everything carefully.
6. Read questions twice.
7. Follow the directions exactly.
8. Use your time wisely.

9. Remember W. A. T. C. H. (see chapter 1).
10. Do the best you can do!

POINTS TO REMEMBER

* Take the practice tests provided on the state's website.
* Spend time studying the explanation of why one answer is correct and the other three answers are wrong. This is a valuable learning strategy.
* For the SAT and ACT, take the preparation courses at the high school.
* Download SAT and ACT practice material onto your own computer. Some are free and others are at a minimal cost.
* Review the techniques learned that best meet your anxiety issues.
* Remember: anxiety causes lower scores on tests than ignorance.
* Take the test; don't let the test take you.

Chapter Twenty-Three

Wind Down and Wrap Up

TEST-TAKING DAY POINTS TO REMEMBER

The easiest way to ensure that all the necessary information is covered is to create a checklist. With the aid of technology, this process is readily available to teachers, parents, and students. The items on these lists help set the tone for a positive and productive testing situation.

FOR THE TEST GIVER

On the day of the test:

1. Read the manual prior to the testing situation, at least twice, so that you know exactly what to say, how many times to say it, and what is timed. (See the explanations of test directions in appendix G.)
2. Set the school telephone and all (teachers' and students') cell phones to "off." This is a must.
3. Put a sign on the classroom door: "Testing—Do Not Disturb."
4. Make sure students understand the directions and what help can and cannot be given. Stress these instructions.
5. Check the answer sheet of each student who has finished and point to the number of any unanswered questions. This may be all the help you are allowed to give.
6. Remind students that they may not know all the answers, especially on national achievement tests.
7. Remind students to read the entire question and all answer choices before selecting their answer.

8. Have extra number-two pencils and erasers handy. I cannot stress this enough.
9. Remind students that if they change their answer, they must erase the first choice completely.
10. Take care of bathroom needs before the test begins.
11. Announce that no one is allowed to enter or leave the room after the test begins.
12. Give stretch breaks and bathroom breaks between sections, if needed.
13. Take notes of the students' demeanor on the day of the test (is the student ill or upset for any reason?).
14. State whether the test is timed and for how long.
15. Remind students of the rules for the test giver:

   - How many times the test giver may read the directions
   - Whether the test giver may explain the directions
   - Whether the test giver can answer specific questions about directions
   - What to do if a student wants to change his or her answer

16. Tell the students what to do if:

   - The pencil breaks
   - A student falls ill
   - The student needs a tissue
   - A student finishes

17. Assure students that they are expected to do their best; alleviate as much pressure as possible.

FOR THE STUDENT

On test-taking day:

1. Read the question and all answer choices before marking the selection.
2. Look for the math sign before completing the problem.
3. Look for the key words in the questions that give clues to the answer.
4. Check to make sure all questions are answered.
5. Guess the answers to questions you do not know, using your guessing skills.
6. Watch the time: don't be a tortoise or a hare.
7. Don't spend a lot of time on one question; skip it and come back to it if time allows. Remember to skip the line on the answer sheet also.

8. For fill-in-the-blank questions, try each answer choice to see which makes the most sense.
9. Expect only one correct answer.
10. Expect no pattern to the answers, such as A B C A B C.
11. Don't worry about the other students.
12. Come prepared with three number-two pencils and an eraser. Again, this is very important.
13. Dress comfortably and for the weather.
14. Read the directions twice.
15. Even if you are sure of the answer on a reading comprehension test, go back and find it in the passage.
16. Be on time. Latecomers are not allowed into a testing room where a test has already begun.
17. Do the best you can!

Appendix A

Definitions of Testing Terms

Achievement test: A test that measures the extent to which a student has attained specific information or mastered specific skills.

Battery: A group of several tests (encompassing the grade-level curriculum) that have been standardized on the same population so that results of the tests are comparable. The most common test batteries are those of achievement tests, which include subtests in all areas of the curriculum.

Composite score: A score that combines several scores.

Correlation: The relationship between two sets of scores or measures.

Criterion referenced test: A test that measures specific knowledge or skills of the student. A criterion referenced test does not rank students against each other or tell if a student is on grade level; it simply tests if the child has mastered specific skills.

Diagnostic test: A test used to diagnose or analyze a student's specific areas of strengths or weaknesses.

Distracter: Any incorrect answer choice in a test.

Grade equivalent: The grade level for which a given score is the real or estimated average.

Item analysis: The process of evaluating single test items with respect to certain characteristics.

Mean: The mean of a set of scores is the average of the scores.

Median: When the scores are ranked from high to low, the median is the middle score.

Norms: Norms are results based on the actual performance of pupils of various grades or ages in the standardized group for the test.

Norm referenced test: This type of test measures what the student knows, compares the student to students of the same age or grade level around the country, and ranks the student against peers.

Objective test: A test scored with a key and consisting of items for which correct responses are determined in advance.

Percentile: A ranking in a distribution of scores. For example, a percentile of eighty-five means that 85 percent of the students who took that test in question scored lower than the student in question. Of every hundred students who took the test in the United States, eighty-four scored lower than the test taker.

Profile: A graphic representation of a student's results on a test. A quick look at a profile will show strengths and weaknesses.

Quartile: When a set of test scores is divided equally into four quarters, each group is a quartile with the top quartile (seventy-fifth percentile to one hundredth percentile) being the best and the bottom (first percentile to twenty-fifth percentile) being the students who need help.

Random sample: A sample of members of a total population chosen in such a way that every member of the population has an equal chance of being included.

Raw score: The number of correct answers, or, in the case of some tests, the number of correct answers minus the number of wrong answers.

Reliability: The extent to which the test measures what it says it is going to measure and is consistent with this measure.

Standard score: The difference between the raw score and the mean, divided by the standard deviation. An example of the classification of standard scores is as follows: Very superior: 130 and up; Superior: 120–129; High average: 110–119; Average: 90–109; Low average: 80–89; Borderline: 70–79; Deficient: 69 and below.

Standardized test: Tests that have the same questions, the same directions for administration, are given in the same setting, and are scored in conformance with definite rules.

Stanine: One of the steps in a nine-point scale of standard scores. For example: Low: 1, 2, 3; Average: 4, 5, 6; High: 7, 8, 9.

Syllabus: An outline of the course of study for a particular component of the school curriculum (e.g., reading, math, social studies, science, etc.).

Validity: The extent to which a test measures what the teacher taught.

Appendix B

Websites of Each State Department of Education

Alabama	http://www.alsde.edu
Alaska	http://www.eed.state.ak.us
Arizona	http://www.ade.state.az.us
Arkansas	http://arkansased.org
California	http://www.cde.ca.gov
Colorado	http://www.cde.state.co.us
Connecticut	http://www.sde.ct.gov/sde/default.asp
Delaware	http://www.doe.state.de.us
District of Columbia	http://dcps.dc.gov/portal/site/DCPS
Florida	http://www.fldoe.org
Georgia	http://www.doe.k12.ga.us
Hawaii	http://www.doe.k12.hi.us
Idaho	http://www.sde.idaho.gov
Illinois	http://www.isbe.state.il.us
Indiana	http://www.doe.in.gov/
Iowa	http://educateiowa.gov/
Kansas	http://www.ksde.org/
Kentucky	http://education.ky.gov/Pages/default.aspx
Louisiana	http://www.doe.state.la.us
Maine	http://www.maine.gov/education/index.shtml

Maryland	http://www.marylandpublicschools.org/msde
Massachusetts	http://www.doe.mass.edu
Michigan	http://www.michigan.gov/mde
Minnesota	http://www.education.state.mn.us
Mississippi	http://www.mde.k12.ms.us
Missouri	http://dese.mo.gov
Montana	http://opi.mt.gov/
Nebraska	http://www.education.ne.gov/
Nevada	http://www.doe.nv.gov/
New Hampshire	http://www.state.nh.us/doe
New Jersey	http://www.state.nj.us/education
New Mexico	http://www.sde.state.nm.us
New York	http://www.nysed.gov
North Carolina	http://www.dpi.state.nc.us
North Dakota	http://www.dpi.state.nd.us
Ohio	http://www.ode.state.oh.us
Oklahoma	http://www.sde.state.ok.us
Oregon	http://www.ode.state.or.us
Pennsylvania	http://www.education.state.pa.us
Rhode Island	http://www.ride.ri.gov/
South Carolina	http://ed.sc.gov/
South Dakota	http://doe.sd.gov
Tennessee	http://www.state.tn.us/education
Texas	http://www.tea.state.tx.us
Utah	http://www.schools.utah.gov/main/
Vermont	http://education.vermont.gov/
Virginia	http://www.doe.virginia.gov/
Washington	http://www.k12.wa.us
West Virginia	http://wvde.state.wv.us
Wisconsin	http://www.dpi.state.wi.us
Wyoming	http://www.k12.wy.us

Appendix C

Game Chart

	1	2	3	4	5	6	7
A							
B							
C							
D							
E							
F							
G							
H							
I							
J							

Appendix D

Suggested Weekly Lesson Plan

MONDAY

Select your skill of the week, and, using the students' materials, write out two sample test questions. Work on these two sample questions step-by-step with the students.

For example, tell students to read the test questions, and then point them to the corresponding passages in their book (reading textbook, library book, social studies textbook). Read the passage to students, alternate reading the passage with students, or have students read it aloud to you. Ask the following question: What is the main idea of the passage?

Discuss each of the four answer choices. Together, discuss why each is a good choice or why it does not answer the question. Repeat this activity with a different passage and a different set of answer choices.

TUESDAY

Follow the same format as Monday using a different source. If the reading text was used Monday, select passages from the social studies or science text on Tuesday.

WEDNESDAY

Follow the same format as Monday and Tuesday, using different material. This time, let students tell you why each choice is right or inappropriate.

THURSDAY

Repeat Wednesday's format.

FRIDAY

Repeat the format for Monday, but have students do the work independently. Check students' work for mastery of the skill. Discuss the results with students.

Daily Lesson Plan

Day: _____
Date: _____
Subject Area: _____
Skill: _____
Textbook: _____ Pages: _____

Sample test item:

Question: _____

_____

Answer choices:

1. _____
2. _____
3. _____
4. _____

Question: _____

_____

Answer choices:

A. _____
B. _____
C. _____
D. _____

Appendix F

Key Words in Test Directions and Questions

TEST DIRECTION VOCABULARY

Children may have difficulty understanding that instructions for a specific task can sometimes be stated in several different ways. For example, test directions use many different commands to tell students to designate the answer: *mark, bubble in, fill in, blacken, color in, shade*, or *darken*. Children may know how to draw a line under but may be thoroughly confused when the directions tell them to select a word that means the same as the underlined word.

Students may prepare for tests by reviewing the material taught in the classroom; by not cramming, which can cause confusion, fatigue, and uncertainty; and by getting adequate rest and nourishment. The next step for students, both before and during a test, is to understand the test directions. Before taking the test, students should become familiar with the following test direction words and their meanings. During the test, they should raise their hand and ask for clarification if needed. In standardized tests, however, the test directions often do not permit clarifications.

Direction vocabulary words can be categorized by the type of test in which they are used. As new federal and state tests are developed, note the direction vocabulary used and add those terms to the following lists.

General:

- Circle, space, oval, shape
- Row
- Not

- Not true, false
- Sample
- Best, most, most likely
- Box
- Probably
- Only
- Diagram
- Corresponding space
- Key words
- Grid
- Graph, chart diagram, table, map, timeline

Reading:

- Passage, story, paragraph, phrase, selection, item
- In this story, refers to, to this passage
- Main idea, mainly about, all about
- Sounds like, rhymes with
- Goes with
- Underlined word or underlined letters
- Describes, tells about
- Punctuation
- Opposite, synonym, antonym
- Sequence, order in which things happen
- Compare, contrast, similar, the same
- Cause, effect

Math:

- *General*

    o Figure, shape, circle
    o Shade, shaded (usually referring to parts of a fraction)
    o Problem, item
    o Equal to, equivalent, another name for
    o Empty set, belonging to a set
    o Solve, work the problem

- *Addition*

    o All together
    o In all
    o Total
    o How many have then
    o Join

     ○ How much

- *Subtraction*

     ○ How many (much) less
     ○ Difference
     ○ How many are left
     ○ Most/more
     ○ Least/less

- *Multiplication*

     ○ Times
     ○ Each
     ○ How many in all

- *Division*

     ○ What fraction, what part
     ○ Divided into
     ○ Divided equally
     ○ Each, how many in one

- *Miscellaneous*

     Beginning, middle, end, next, finally, last
     Top, bottom
     Before, after
     Over, under, above, below
     Choice
     None, none of these, none of the above, not here
     In real life, cannot really happen
     Diagram, table, chart, graph
     Makes sense
     Bold face, italics, dark print
     Best tells
     Stands for, the same as, another way of saying, almost the same as, closest
     In meaning to, refers to
     Next to, next, down, beside

Social Studies:

- Locate (on a map or other graphic)
- Function of
- Terms found in the glossary of the classroom textbook

Science:

- Demonstrates
- Characteristics
- Cell
- Organism
- Terms found in the glossary of the classroom textbook

Notes

1. TEST-WISENESS: WHAT, WHEN, WHY, AND HOW

1. Divine, James H., & Kylen, David W., 1979, *How to Beat Test Anxiety*, New York: Barron's Educational Series.
2. Scruggs, Thomas E., & Mastropieri, Margo A., 1992, *Teaching Test-Taking Skills*, Cambridge, MA: Brookline Books.

6. TECHNIQUES: THE ANXIETY FACTOR

1. Cizek, Gregory J., & Burg, Samantha S., 2006, *Addressing Test Anxiety in a High-Stakes Environment*, Thousand Oaks, CA: Corwin Press.
2. Durham, Guinevere M., 1983, *A Program to Alleviate Test Anxiety in Students, Teachers, and Parents through Inservice and Test Taking Techniques: A Doctoral Practicum in Early Childhood Education*, Ft. Lauderdale, FL: Nova University.

8. STYLES OF LEARNING

1. Buzan, Tony, 1991, *Use Both Sides of Your Brain*, London, England: A Plume Book (Penguin Group).
2. Rose, Colin, 1985, Wrote *Accelerated Learning* Reading Program for Schools.
3. The District of Columbia Public Schools, 1986-1987, *Early Learning and Early Identification Follow-Up Study: Transition from the Early to Later Childhood Grades*, Washington, DC: Center for Systemic Educational Change.

References

CHAPTER 1

1. Divine, James H., & Kylen, David W. 1979. *How to Beat Test Anxiety*. New York: Barron's Educational Series, Inc.

   Dr. Divine, Ed.D Educational Psychology, has taught several college-level courses in the field of education, particularly in research and measurement and assessment. His primary research was in learning, teaching, development, and assessment.

   David Kylen was a joint author of this book and has a similar background and interests. They also co-authored *How to Beat Test Anxiety and Score Higher on the SAT and All Other Exams* (1982).

2. Scruggs, Thomas E., & Mastropieri, Margo A. 1992. *Teaching Test-Taking Skills*. Cambridge, MA: Brookline Books.

   Both authors are on the special education faculty of Perdue University. The book was revised in 2000. These authors also joined forces in several other books in the field of special education, instruction, and test-taking skills.

CHAPTER 6

1. Cizek, Gregory J., & Burg, Samantha S. 2006. *Addressing Test Anxiety in a High-Stakes Environment*. Thousand Oaks, CA: Corwin Press.

   Gregory Cizek is a professor of education measurement at the University of North Carolina.

   Samantha Burg is a doctoral student in educational psychology, measurement, and evaluation at the University of North Carolina.

2. Durham, Guinevere M. 1983. *A Program to Alleviate Test Anxiety in Students, Teachers, and Parents through Inservice and Test-Taking Techniques*. Doctoral practicum in

early childhood education (a two-year study of research, implementation, and evaluation of test-taking techniques in elementary schools). Ft. Lauderdale, FL: Nova University.

CHAPTER 8

1. Buzan, Tony. 1991. *Use Both Sides of Your Brain*. London, England: A Pluma Book (Penguin Group).

   Tony Buzan has done extensive research on the working of the human brain. He is one of the world's leading authorities on learning techniques, and his book provides step-by-step exercises for discovering the powers of using the right side of the brain and learning to use the left side of the brain more effectively.

2. Rose, Colin, 1987. Developed the *Accelerated Learning* Reading Program for Schools.

3. The District of Columbia Public Schools. 1986–1987. *Early Learning and Early Identification Follow-Up Study: Transition from the Early to the Later Childhood Grades*. Washington, DC: Center for Systemic Educational Change.

   The report was compiled during 1990–1993 by Rebecca A. Marcon. She is a developmental psychologist and professor at the University of North Florida, Jacksonville, Florida.

ADDITIONAL REFERENCES OF INTEREST

Alford, Robert L. 1979. *Tips on Testing: Strategies for Test Taking*. Washington, DC: University Press of America.

Burrill, Lois E. 1981. *How a Standardized Achievement Test Is Built*. Test Service Notebook 125. New York: Psychological Corporation.

Feder, Bernard. 1979. *The Complete Guide to Taking Tests*. Englewood Cliffs, NJ: Prentice-Hall.

Florida Department of Education. 1981. *Item Development Workshop*. Tallahassee: State of Florida, Department of State.

Lang, Bob. 1981. "Promoting Test-Wiseness." *Journal of Reading* 24 (8): 740–42.

About the Author

Guinevere Durham has been described by one of her teachers as an "advocate of children." She has spent thirty years in every aspect of elementary and early childhood education, confronting challenges and reaping blessings. She also was a willing participant in the educational and social activities of her six children. Her education and experiences instilled in her the need to help both teachers and children. Thus, the purpose for *Teaching Test-Taking Skills*.

Durham has won national awards as a teacher of the year and educator of the year. In addition, she was recognized for her teacher workshops and conference presentations in the fields of parenting, school improvement, and test-taking strategies. Her contributions to publishers of reading textbooks and Sunday school curricula benefited teachers in their efforts to help students. As a retired elementary principal with a bachelor's and master's degrees in elementary education and a doctorate in early childhood education, she has qualified for listings in three different *Who's Who* in education during her career.